CW00547822

Baptist Theology

Stephen R. Holmes

Published by T&T Clark International
A Continuum Imprint
The Tower Building, 11 York Road, London SE1 7NX
80 Maiden Lane, Suite 704, New York, NY 10038

www.continuumbooks.com

British Library Cataloguing-in-Publication Data
A catalogue record for this book is available from the British Library

ISBN HB: 978-0-567-65097-9
PB: 978-0-567-00031-6

Typeset by Deanta Global Publishing Services, Chennai, India
Printed and bound in India

For the students and staff of Spurgeons College, past and present.

'Et teneo, et teneor'

Contents

Acknowledgements

One of the themes of this book is the importance of the local congregation for Baptists. I have learnt much about Baptist theology from the congregations that have allowed me to minister among them in one role or another, and it is a pleasure to thank them for their graciousness, for their love and forgiveness, and for all they have taught me on this subject, and on many others, over the years: Ramsden Road Baptist Church; West Wickham and Shirley Baptist Church; Ashford (Middlesex) Baptist Church; and St Andrews Baptist Church.

From time to time I have had the privilege of working on aspects of Baptist theology in order to serve a local association or denomination. I am grateful for all such invitations and particularly for the people I have worked with. Paul Fiddes, Faith Bowers, Sean Winter, Anthony Cross and Myra Blyth particularly come to mind, but there have been many others. Theological reflection is rich in British Baptist life presently, with three sponsored lectures (the Baptist Historical Society lecture, the Beasley-Murray lecture and the Whitley lecture, all of which I have been privileged to give), an ongoing series of conferences for ministers engaged in the work of theology and the Scottish Baptist Theological Society, all making a significant contribution. By attending and giving lectures and conference papers I have gained much; there are too many people to thank, but interactions with Ruth Goldbourne, Andrew Rollinson and Jim Gordon particularly stand out in my mind.

I have had the privilege of talking to or working with several other scholars and with several interested students over the years on this theme and I am thankful to them all: Paul Fiddes, Nigel Wright, John Colwell, Ian Randall, David Bebbington, John Coffey, Chris Chun, Jason Sexton, Shawn Bawulski, Christian George, Ian Birch, Andy Goodliff and Jeff Oldfield. Paul Fiddes and Curtis Freeman read this book in draft and were kind enough to make very helpful suggestions for improvements. Any errors and all interpretations of course remain entirely my responsibility.

I remain more grateful than words can say to Heather and immensely proud of our three daughters, Judith, Philippa and Elspeth.

I first began to reflect seriously on Baptist theology while training for ministry at Spurgeon's College in London. There I was taught by, and then later had the privilege of working alongside, Nigel Wright, John Colwell, Ian Randall, Stuart Murray-Williams and Michael Quicke, among several others. Equally important in shaping mind, character and life were my fellow students and the students I later taught at Spurgeons. The College Conference, composed of past and present students and staff, has done me the honour of electing me its president for 2012–13; this book is dedicated to those sisters and brothers, who live out the calling of Baptist theology in personal lives and church communities on a day-to-day basis. Everything I know of who they are and what they do confirms my belief that their ministries are a far more eloquent testimony to the glories of the Baptist vision than anything I could write.

Stephen R. Holmes
On the 250th anniversary of the birth of William Carey
St Andrews

Introduction

Baptist Theology?

Baptists form the largest Protestant denomination in the world today, numbering over 100 million members spread across each continent. Theologically, however, they have been much less significant than their numbers might suggest. Baptists have contributed at the very highest level in biblical scholarship, missiology and areas of practical theology; a list of the hundred greatest theologians of the modern period, however, would not feature many, if any, Baptist names, and those that were there would not be very near the top. There are reasons for this, which I explore later in this book, but it raises, or perhaps illustrates, a further problem that needs to be addressed from the start.

Other titles in this series can point to and build upon a rich tradition of authorized confessional dogmatic material. 'Catholic theology' is defined in important ways by the contents of the catechism and the authoritative documents of the magisterium; the expositor of 'Reformed theology' can point to a tradition of confessional statements and commentary upon them; while there are a number of Baptist confessional documents, they have never given birth to any significant school of interpretation and commentary. 'Baptist theology' does not exist in the way that 'Reformed theology' does, even if individual theologians do sometimes try to be self-consciously 'Baptist' in the way that they do their work.

(There has been a recent trend to claim a tradition of 'baptist theology,' or 'baptistic theology' – in either case the lower-case 'b' denotes that this tradition goes wider than historically Baptist churches to include other believers' church traditions, notably the various Anabaptist churches. On this telling, the lack of major scholarly theologians demonstrates the success of baptist theology, in that, for the believers' church, reflection on the gospel is something that only properly belongs to the local congregation, and should not be located in academy or seminary. This is an interesting and significant development, but it does not seem to me that there is yet a credible historical claim that this is the authentic Baptist tradition – rather, it is a recent representation of one particular emphasis within that tradition.)

An introduction to Baptist theology, then, is inevitably both partial and creative. Partial because the writer inevitably comes from a particular perspective: I write as a Baptist, baptized and ordained within the Baptist Union of Great Britain, and presently accredited as a minister within the Baptist Union of Scotland. I am acutely conscious that my British context colours the way I reflect on Baptist theology (as well as the way I spell 'colours'). This is of course true in terms of knowledge: I understand the British Baptist tradition from within; all other traditions I have had to learn. It is, however, true at more basic levels than that: at the most visceral level, even when fully aware of the divergent practices of different Baptist traditions and the history which led to them, I am acutely conscious that some things feel normal, 'Baptist,' to me, and other things feel strange and alien. Wherever I have been conscious, or even suspicious, of such bias, I have sought to overcome it; no doubt at times I have failed; no doubt that at other times, through ignorance, I have allowed bias to intrude without being aware that what seems normal to me is in fact rather odd and distinctive. My and any account of Baptist theology is thus 'partial' in the sense that it is inevitably incomplete.

Even in full possession of the facts and untainted by bias, however, any account of Baptist theology presently penned will be partial in the other sense of that word ('partial' as the opposite of 'impartial', rather than as the opposite of 'complete'): lacking a (even relatively) united body of reflection that is generally agreed to make up the discourse of 'Baptist theology', the writer must make his or her own judgements about what is central, and what peripheral, to the tradition, and so must essay an interpretation which intentionally imposes a particular shape on the material, all the while conscious that other judgements could have been made. To take only one example, this is already evident in the decision over where a history of Baptist theology might start: is it a story of a particular development of the Calvinist tradition, via the English Separatists, thus locating Baptist theology in its origin at least as a subset of Reformed theology,[1] as was often assumed by Baptist writers in the nineteenth century? Is it a story of a broader believers' church tradition, beginning with the Radical Reformation rather than with Calvin and Bullinger, and developing in dialogue with other radical traditions, as contemporary advocates of the 'baptist theology' model would insist? Or is it a story of the continuation of the true (Baptist) churches, founded by Jesus, often driven underground by oppression from false churches, but never quite extinguished, as an American Landmarkist tradition would teach?

I take it that, in purely historical terms, one needs to begin the story with a particular branch of the English Separatist tradition, and so trace the main narrative of the story back to the influence of Calvin, Bucer and Bullinger on the English Reformation. That said, the decisive rejection – already among the Separatists, before the question of believers' baptism had ever been raised – of any union between church leadership and state authority locates the Baptists from the first within a radical tradition which invites certain theological positions, including (but not limited to) believers' baptism itself, an account of Christ's reign over the church as unmediated and a profound suspicion of state coercion. It is no surprise, then, to find a family resemblance with other believers' church (or 'baptistic') traditions, even when there is no evidence of direct influence, and no surprise either to find a recognition of shared values, even if sometimes in the face of serious disagreements, when other believers' church traditions are encountered.

Similarly, an introduction to Baptist theology has to be creative, simply because there is no settled tradition to summarize and report. One might, variously, summarize the respective theologies of Benjamin Keach, Isaac Backus, John Gill, Jim McClendon, Stan Grenz, Carl Henry, Paul Fiddes or Nigel Wright – but there is no settled account of what links these figures together (and excludes sympathetic, but non-Baptist [and non-baptist], fellow-travellers such as John Owen or Stanley Hauerwas). The writer of a Baptist theology has to propose his or her own account, and any proposed account will need exposition and defence, and will be open to challenge.

This is not to say that there are not proposals on the table, but none has yet achieved anything like consensus status, and none seems, to me, adequate to account for the variety of the movement. I have already noted the focus on a shared believers' church heritage, locating the task of theology, and the core of Christian experience, in the local church. This 'baptistic' account of Baptist theology succeeds in capturing some crucial Baptist distinctives, notably an intense focus on the local congregation as the central context for faith and life, and a commitment to faith as something lived, not something merely theoretical. It appears to have less to say, however, about the remarkable consistency with which Baptists across the world and down through the centuries have formed associations of churches, about the place of the Bible in Baptist life, or indeed about the practice of believers' baptism. The centrality of the local congregation of believers will be important for my account of Baptist theology, but other themes must supplement it for an adequate account to be offered.

Another proposal, presently popular in Southern Baptist thought in the US, claims that Baptists are distinctive in that they are the purest evangelicals. What sets Baptists apart from all others is the consistency of their obedience to Scripture on every point. Congregational government, a focus on congregational life, believers' baptism, associationalism and every other Baptist distinctive – all are clearly taught in Scripture and it is, essentially, the faithlessness of others which prevents them from being Baptist. For an example of this position, consider Bush and Nettles, who comment, rather coolly, that '[w]e could wish that all evangelical Christians would search the Scriptures and thus prove what is true faith and practice'.[2] Others are not Baptists because they are insufficiently committed to Biblical authority, or because they have not troubled themselves to discover the clear teaching of Scripture. Certainly this suggestion chimes with the Baptist tradition in its origins and in much of its development: Baptists believed that they had adequately recovered primitive apostolic practice, and that others were either refusing to listen to the plain testimony of Scripture, or deliberately refusing to follow that testimony out of a misplaced desire not to disrupt the peace of the church or similar.

However, is such an account really credible today? On the one hand, the confidence with which we once believed we could read particular church orders – whatever they may be – from the New Testament text is almost entirely eroded, in serious Biblical scholarship at least. On the other, particularly from the perspective of British Baptist life, where significant involvement with a broader evangelicalism has been normal, the suggestion that other evangelicals are less serious in their commitment to Scripture than Baptist evangelicals appears rather ridiculous, and indeed borders on the offensive. That said, there can be no denying the importance of the Bible to Baptist theology, and a biblicist theme inevitably runs throughout my exposition in this book.

An earlier suggestion for the centre of Baptist theology, also originating in Southern Baptist life but now more naturally found among non-Southern Baptist Convention (SBC) Baptists in the US, takes E.Y. Mullins's suggestion that 'soul competency' is the distinctive Baptist vision. In the good providence of God, each person is granted the ability and the responsibility of responding to God's call. The individual does not need priest nor bishop nor church nor community to respond adequately to God. The immediate consequence of this for Mullins is a profound commitment to religious liberty, which has certainly been a lasting feature of Baptist witness down the centuries, and is always claimed as a core distinctive in accounts of Baptist theology. Mullins's account, however, perhaps fails in the opposite direction to the 'baptistic' vision, in so stressing the individual that it does not adequately account for the place of the local church in Baptist theology. I confess also to a profound unhappiness with the term 'soul competency,' which seems to me to grant far too much spiritual capacity to the fallen human heart; I say more about Mullins, and explore both these criticisms more fully, in Chapter 6 below.

A fourth proposal, originating in recent British Baptist reflection, is that the notion of covenant might provide a useful organizing motif for Baptist theology. 'Covenant' was a significant theme in seventeenth-century theology, specifying both the ways in which God has promised to manifest salvation to the people, and the solemn act of people covenanting together before God for a particular, holy, purpose (the most famous example might be the Solemn League and Covenant, formed between Scots Presbyterians and the English Parliament to oppose King Charles I). Early Baptist churches were often formed by a formal covenant made between the members, and this was seen as central to ecclesial identity and faithfulness. By locating such ecclesial covenant-making as a part of God's covenant of salvation, the early Baptists brought their ecclesial convictions about the importance of the local congregation into their doctrine of God's salvific work.

Covenant was certainly a significant theme for seventeenth-century Baptists (but then it was for seventeenth-century Presbyterians as well), and an account such as that above helpfully links a focus on the local congregation with central theological themes, helping us to understand why Baptist theology is so eccel-sially focused; that said, it seems to me that, historically speaking, covenant ceases to be an important concept for most Baptists by the beginning of the eighteenth century, and so claiming it as *the* central motif in Baptist theology is rather ambitious.

My proposal for an organizing theme for Baptist theology learns from each of these approaches, but I hope it is more encompassing than any of them. I begin by suggesting that there are two foci around which Baptist life is lived: the individual believer and the local church. On the one hand, the practice of believers' baptism demonstrates an intense individualism,[3] a focus on the belief that God deals directly with each particular human person; on the other hand, the Baptist stress on the significance of the local congregation provides a focus on that community as the context in which God has promised to be active. Theologically, God's work in each of these poles needs to be described Christologically and pneumatologically. Christ alone has the right to command the individual conscience, which means both that every particular person is responsible for their own religious decisions and practices, and that state interference in, or legislation for, religious belief and/or practice should never be permitted. Faith and regeneration are always a miracle of grace, dependent on the atoning sacrifice of Christ and made actual in each individual life through the present work of the Holy Spirit; believers' baptism is (at least) a powerful witness to this pneumatological regeneration.

Turning to the second pole, the local church, I wish to argue that the particular Baptist vision of the local church depends, theologically, on the belief that Christ's rule over the church is experienced directly by each local congregation, and not mediated through a translocal hierarchy. Christ is directly present wherever his people are gathered – congregated – in his name, and Christ's presence guarantees the reality and adequacy of the church. In seeking to know and discover the call of Christ on its life, however, each local church is dependent on the Spirit's aid and guidance, which is ordinarily experienced in gathered community. This is the church meeting, and the reason for the primacy of the church meeting in Baptist decision-making is that this is the place where the church can expect the Spirit to reveal the mind of Christ.

These two poles are not in tension in Baptist theology – or, rather, they can be in particular contexts and instances, but there is no necessary tension – but neither may be lost without losing the heart of the vision. God, through the Son and the Spirit, calls individual believers into covenanted relationship in the local church, and equips them to build up one another within the local church, and to hear and obey the ongoing missional call to make every other human person a believer. This is Baptist theology.

In this, I am taking a middle ground on what is perhaps the most crucial debate in determining the nature of Baptist theology: its distance from other Christian traditions. Some accounts of Baptist theology – the 'baptist' believers' church position noted above, and the Landmarkist claim that only Baptists are true Christians – have a 'maximal' account of the distance of Baptist theology from other theological traditions: there are points of contact, but, fundamentally, Baptists (or baptists) have a distinct and different theological genius which other traditions have little or no insight into, and so Baptist Christianity is markedly and decisively separated from other visions of Christianity. Alternatively, it is possible to have a 'minimal' account of this distance: Baptists are evangelicals with a particular baptismal practice, or another strand of the Reformed movement; a couple of very visible and distinctive ecclesial practices should not blind us to the fundamental continuity of Baptists with other Christian groups.

I accept that Baptists share in a broader Christian (specifically, Reformed and evangelical) heritage, and that on most theological issues, this shared heritage is decisive: there is no Baptist doctrine of the Trinity, or of salvation, or of eschatology, which is not shared with other Christian communities (I discuss this in Chapter 4). I therefore find a 'maximal' account of the distance between Baptists and others unconvincing. However, on the particular issue of ecclesiology, it seems to me that there are distinctive Baptist (or perhaps baptist) positions which seriously affect the shapes of arguments that can be accepted in Baptist life. On ecclesiological questions which we currently face alongside other Christian traditions, often we need to find distinctive arguments of our own, because our vision of what it is to be Christ's church is sufficiently different from others to make the easy sharing of arguments impossible.[4]

The book is organized as follows: three chapters describe the history of the Baptist movement, with a particular focus on intellectual history. Chapter 1 looks at Baptists in Britain from their beginnings until 1800; Chapter 2 considers Baptists in America; Chapter 3 concludes the British story and tells the history of Baptists in Europe, Australia and in the majority world. In Chapter 4, I note that on most central doctrines – Trinity, Christology, eschatology and so forth – there is no distinctive Baptist theology, a point I demonstrate by briefly exploring the distinctive but varied contributions of Baptist theologians to these various topics. Chapter 5 is my first exposition of the ecclesiology that is at the heart of Baptist theology, expounding the two poles of individualism and congregationalism through a consideration of believers' baptism and congregational government. I also locate Baptist ecclesiology in the context of ecumenical ecclesiological discussions. Chapter 6 explores the historically central Baptist conviction of religious liberty by locating it theologically, as an expression of the lordship of Christ over the conscience ('the crown rights of the Redeemer,' in the fine old phrase of John Knox); here I also examine more recent transformations of the same idea, such as Mullins's account of 'soul competency'. Chapter 7 turns to mission and holiness as particular emphases in a Baptist theology of the Christian life, and tries to narrate both within the broad outline of Baptist theology that I have sought to develop. Chapter 8 draws the threads together in a brief conclusion.

James Bruton Gambrell, sometime president of both Mercer University and the Southern Baptist Convention, is commonly credited with these stirring words:

> God's Word is plain. A Baptist has only to read and obey. He need not be a scholar, or a philosopher, though he may be both. He has no trouble to explain away what is written.

> He can read it and go by it without embarrassment. He can afford to be plain, simple, straightforward, and obedient, knowing that if there is anything wrong with the teaching of the New Testament, he is not to blame for it. I am a Baptist because John was, Jesus was, the apostles were, the first churches were, and all the world ought to be![5]

I confess to not sharing Gambrell's serene confidence in the simple correctness of our shared denominational heritage. Humanly speaking, I am a Baptist because the university friend who was tasked with disciplining me after my conversion at a Christian Union mission happened to be attending the local Baptist church at that point, although himself an Anglican. Discovering a call to ministry within that context, I naturally candidated for Baptist ministry. I am convinced of the rightness of certain central Baptist principles – notably the unmediated Lordship of Christ over each individual conscience and over each gathered congregation – and I find in them, and in their development, a creative, vibrant and distinctive expression of Christian faith and life that seems worthy of exploration and exposition. This book is a part of that work, offered not because I believe that the entire world ought to be Baptists, but because I believe we have a vision of the Christian life that is of interest and worth, and that deserves to be better understood – by Baptists, and by others – than it presently is.

Chapter 1
Baptist Beginnings

2009 saw celebrations of the four-hundredth anniversary of the Baptist movement. However, to understand the movement, and particularly its theological development, we need to go further back into history still. Perhaps the story should begin with the birth of the Church at Pentecost, fifty days after the resurrection of Jesus Christ; there is an influential tradition of Baptist life that would take it even further back than that, exemplified by a classic piece of Baptist doggerel from nineteenth-century America:

> Not at the Jordan River,
> But in that flowing stream,
> Stood John the Baptist Preacher,
> When he baptizèd Him.
> John was a Baptist preacher,
> When he baptized the Lamb,
> So Jesus was a Baptist,
> And thus the Baptists came.[1]

This tradition of asserting that the Baptist movement is the authentic continuation of New Testament Christianity will become important at several points in the story that follows. Sober historical judgement and the constraints of space suggest that the story be started a little later than John's baptism of Jesus, however, with the Protestant Reformation of the sixteenth century.

The English Reformation and the Separatist Movement

The history of the Reformation in England was particularly messy for a variety of reasons. Henry VIII and Thomas Cromwell

(Henry's chief minister 1532–40) were certainly united in a desire to purge the English church of abuses and scandals, but were at least as interested in bringing the church under the control of the state. On 1 May 1532, Henry famously commented (to a gathering of parliamentarians) 'we thought that the clergy of our realm had been our subjects wholly, but now we have well perceived that they be but half our subjects ... for all the prelates ... make an oath to the Pope, clean contrary to the oath that they make to us, so that they seem to be his subjects, not ours.'[2]

Cromwell steered a series of Acts through parliament in 1534, removing powers to appoint to ecclesiastical office in England from the Pope, securing the king's right to appoint bishops and making the king the supreme head of the English church. Henry appointed Cromwell his vice-regent, and Cromwell set about reorganizing the church in far-reaching ways, securing his favour with the king by increasing vastly the taxes collected from the clergy. There were doctrinal and liturgical reforms; Coverdale's English translation of the Bible was licensed, and was to be available for reading in every parish church. However, the comparison with Scotland, and the wholesale establishment of a Reformed national church there in the mid-sixteenth century, demonstrates how partial and particular the reforms in England were. In 1543, an Act was passed limiting the reading of the English Bible to the upper classes.

In 1547, Henry died and was succeeded by his nine-year-old son, Edward VI. Edward was to reign only six years before he died, and his royal power was effectively administered by his 'Protectors', first the Earl of Hertford (soon to become the Duke of Somerset), and then the Earl of Warwick (who became the Duke of Northumberland). Under the rule of Edward's Protectors, a more thorough policy of reform was carried through, resulting in the issuing of Cranmer's prayer-books and articles of religion. There was no relaxation of the state's control on the church in these reforms; indeed, a number of groups who might be seen as proto-Baptist (mostly immigrant Anabaptists from the Netherlands, as far as we can tell) were vigorously persecuted. When Edward died, however, despite an attempt to secure a

Protestant succession through Lady Jane Grey, Queen Mary took the throne and attempted to return the country to the old Roman Catholic liturgies and traditions.

Queen Mary's brutal and inept attempts to restore the old faith lasted only a little over five years before her own death in 1558. Nonetheless, her reign is decisive for the events that led to the birth of the Baptist movement half a century later. On the one hand, many convinced Protestants – perhaps as many as a thousand – spent the five years of her rule in exile in Protestant states on the continent, forming local congregations which developed in different ways, depending on the leaders of the group, and the conversations they were able to have with local church leaders, such as Calvin or Bullinger. On the other hand, particularly in the south east of England, and supremely in London, the almost—routine spectacle of state-sponsored brutality in the name of established religion (in three years, almost 300 people were burnt to death as heretics) must have fuelled unhappiness with the imposition of particular forms of religion by the state.

Mary was succeeded by her half-sister Elizabeth, whose reign would last almost forty years, until her death in 1603. Elizabeth returned England to Protestantism, but of a deliberately moderate kind. She was a consummate politician, and it would seem that in the early years she gave more than she would have liked to the returning exiles to ensure their support. As her own position became more secure, she pursued her own determined policy of creating a moderately reformed church, of which she would be supreme governor, and in which there would be uniformity of liturgy and practice. The church was rigorously controlled, and religious dissidents who presumed to preach without license from the local bishop, for example, could expect to find themselves closely monitored and sometimes imprisoned.

Elizabeth's ecclesiastical policy was designed to minimize opposition; the rapid imposition of reform under Edward, and the brutal reversion to Catholicism under Mary, had alike led to serious civil unrest. Elizabeth sought a middle position which she hoped would be acceptable to all of her subjects. Some of the returned exiles, however, had developed a willingness to stand up against the government of the day in the name of religious duty, and a vision, or a variety of visions, of what a truly biblical church should look like. A series of controversies, often over apparently trivial matters such as what should be worn when celebrating the Eucharist, tested Elizabeth's resolve to maintain uniformity and control.

Under Elizabeth, then, a new religious phenomenon began: separatism. The Separatists refused to compromise on matters of religious practice, and formed their own, illegal, congregations where they could worship according to their own consciences, rather than according to the dictates of the state. Their convictions and practices were varied, and the congregations would often split over disagreements, leading to a series of factions, the most significant being the Brownists and Barrowists. Whichever faction is in view, however, the heart of their complaint was always ecclesiological. They were interested in what a church should be, according to New Testament teaching, and found the established churches wanting on this measure.

This obsession with correct church order can seem rather odd to the modern reader, but it was ubiquitous in the sixteenth and seventeenth centuries. The Church of England's own Ordinal asserted that '[i]t is evident unto all men, diligently readinge holye scripture, and auncient aucthours, that from the Apostles tyme, there hathe bene these orders of Ministers in Christes church, Bisshoppes, Priestes, and Deacons'.[3] For the Separatists, a different church order was evident from reading Scripture (and the testimony of 'ancient authors' was of little interest); the notion that Scripture commanded a particular model of churchmanship, however, was shared by all sides of the argument, and the Separatist desire was to obey Scripture.

While Separatist congregational practice was illegal under Elizabeth's rule, brutal persecution was, in practice, relatively rare – the hanging of Greenwood, Barrow and Penry in 1593 stands out as a fairly isolated instance. More commonly, Separatists were first imprisoned, and then, if they refused to return to the established church, exiled. Nonetheless, by the time Elizabeth died, and James VI of Scotland came to the throne of England (as James I of England) in 1603, many Separatists were looking to the toleration of the Netherlands for a temporary or permanent home. The most famous of these exiled Separatist congregations is undoubtedly that of John Robinson, which supplied the 'pilgrim fathers' who would sail on the Mayflower to found a colony in Massachusetts in 1620. Robinson had come to Separatist convictions and left his parish ministry in 1606; he joined with a pair of linked Separatist congregations in Gainsborough and Scrooby, north west of Lincoln, which had been founded by Richard Clyfton, another former clergyman, two years before, and had divided for reasons of safety, rather than schism. Clyfton became pastor in Scrooby, to be succeeded by Robinson; the pastor and elder of the Gainsborough congregation were, respectively, John Smyth and Thomas Helwys, the two acknowledged founders of the Baptist movement.

Soon both the Scrooby and Gainsborough congregations emigrated to the Netherlands. Both initially arrived in Amsterdam; Robinson then took the Scrooby congregation to Leyden, where he settled and died; Smyth and Helwys continued to meet in Amsterdam, where they initially joined with another exiled Separatist congregation, the Barrowist congregation under Francis Johnson. Smyth soon quarrelled with Johnson over the New Testament teaching on church officers, however, and in consequence formed a separate congregation.

The Beginnings of the Baptist Movement

Baptism was already a live question for these Separatists. There was a long-standing debate within their tradition over the validity of baptism administered by an Anglican clergyman – they agreed that it was necessarily baptism administered by a false minister in a false church, but did that make it invalid? It is no surprise, then, that Smyth's new congregation was studying the New Testament teaching on baptism with this question in mind. The conclusion they drew, however, was radical within their tradition: not just Anglican baptism, but all baptism of infants, was invalid according to the Scriptures. Baptism was only properly administered to one who had confessed his or her own faith and expressed the desire to follow Jesus in the company of the church. Finding no true church to receive this true baptism from, as Robinson reports, in 1609 'Mr Smith [*sic*] baptized first himself and next Mr Helwys and so the rest'. The Baptist movement was born.[4]

This belief about baptism, although seemingly previously unknown in English church traditions, was not in fact totally novel. A number of groups and individuals in the continental Reformation traditions had come to similar beliefs about baptism, and indeed about the inappropriateness of the state imposing particular forms of religion. Collectively, these groups are known as Anabaptists. Many of them had other novel beliefs, ranging from the eccentric to the heretical, and they were routinely and brutally persecuted across Europe. A violent revolutionary group sharing some similar beliefs had established a city-state in Munster in Germany in the mid-1530s; their eccentricities stretched to polygamy, and their brutality became legendary. While many – perhaps most – Anabaptists were pacifists and broadly orthodox, Munster became the visible face of the movement, and persecution was redoubled. Only a few groups survived, the most significant of which were the Mennonites, followers of Menno Simons, in the Netherlands.

There is no direct evidence of influence of the Mennonites on Smyth and Helwys, or on earlier generations of English Separatists. However, there was a Mennonite Waterlander congregation in Amsterdam when Smyth and Helwys arrived there, and it is noticeable that many of the earlier Separatist leaders, including Robert Browne, lived or worked in places such as Norwich, with significant Dutch immigrant populations, presumably including some with sympathy for, or knowledge of, Mennonite beliefs. Surprisingly, the most likely influence of the Waterlanders on Smyth is not baptism – the ongoing debates make it entirely plausible that he was thinking about that issue – but his decision, at about the same time, to embrace Arminian beliefs. The Separatists were traditionally Calvinist, believing that God predestined certain people to salvation and others to reprobation; Smyth came to believe instead that God offers salvation to all people, and that we have the ability to accept or reject the offer. This, Arminian, position was not unique to the Mennonites, but they might be the most plausible source of Smyth's discovering it.

Smyth soon after became convinced that the Mennonite congregation was a true church, and sought union between his congregation and it; Helwys and about ten others opposed the move. (This division is again indicative of the preoccupation with ecclesiology among the Separatists: Smyth, perceiving a true church in existence, believed he had no option but to join it; separation from a true church was not an option.) Helwys drew up a confession of faith, stating Arminian beliefs and then going on to describe in some detail his understanding of the nature of the church. He also became convinced that it was a Christian duty not to flee persecution but to witness steadfastly to Christ in the midst of it, and so he and his little congregation returned to England in 1612, announcing their presence in a book dedicated to King James, Helwys's *Short Declaration of the Mystery of Iniquity*, the first plea for general religious tolerance in the English language. The plea inevitably fell on deaf ears, and Helwys was to die in prison four years later.

For three decades Helwys's followers continued underground in England. It seems that John Murton became their pastor, publishing further pleas for general tolerance, and a defence of Arminianism. The group split over unrecorded Christological differences around 1624, with Elias Tookey leading fifteen others to form a separate congregation. By 1626, alongside the two London congregations, there were congregations in Lincoln, Sarum, Coventry and Tiverton, containing something over 150 members between them. We have no records from the 1630s, but in the mid-1640s we hear, via a scandalized opponent, of a popular and lively fellowship meeting at Bell Alley, Coleman Street, in London, under the ministry of Thomas Lambe. It seems reasonable to assume that this is the direct descendent of the congregation founded by Helwys and pastored by Murton.

A seemingly unconnected development led to the founding of Calvinistic Baptist churches in London in the same period. These had their roots in a congregation begun by Henry Jacob in 1616. Jacob had been a prominent proponent of further reform of the Church of England, and had been imprisoned and banished for his views. By 1616 he was, however, rather moderate compared to other Separatists: he was not opposed to the continued existence of the state church, and even recognized parish churches as true churches, but he argued that there should be space for other congregations to worship and live in ways they considered more adequate than those found within the national church.

Jacob was succeeded as pastor by John Lathrop, who was in turn succeeded by Henry Jessey in 1637. During this time there were various splits and reunions. Two of the daughter congregations are of particular interest: in 1633 a group separated as a result of a debate over whether it had been appropriate for a member of the congregation to have a child baptized in the parish church. This group was soon to be led by Samuel Eaton, who had received 'a further baptism' – although whether this was because he doubted the validity of infant baptism *per se*, or merely of baptism performed in the Church of England, is not clear. By 1638, however, Eaton was clearly convinced that baptism should be administered to believers only.

In that same year, a further group separated from the main Jessey congregation to form a church under John Spilsbury. This congregation required belief in believers' baptism. In 1640, a member of Jessey's congregation, Richard Blunt, became convinced that baptism should be an act of immersion. Jessey took to immersing infants; Blunt himself however (re-)baptized more than fifty believers from the church. In 1642, Hanserd Knollys, a former clergyman, requested of the church that his child not be baptized. Jessey's congregation finally came to accept a variety of baptismal practices (with Jessey himself accepting believers' baptism in 1645), but a new, Baptist, church, which Knollys joined, began as a result of the debate, under the leadership of William Kiffin. In 1644, a Confession of Faith was drawn up and signed by ministers and representatives of seven Calvinistic Baptist churches in London, including Spilsbury and Kiffin. By the middle of the century, then, there was a small network of Arminian (or 'General') Baptist churches across England, and a smaller network of Calvinist (or 'Particular') Baptist churches in London.

Did these churches have a distinctive theological vision beyond believers' baptism? There are reasons to suppose that they did, in at least two ways. On the one hand, although they came from a notoriously independent, and indeed fissiparous, movement in English Separatism, they seemed to temper this with a commitment to finding common cause between congregations. Whitley's claim that '[f]rom the beginning Baptists were not "Independents"; they always sought for fellowship between the different churches'[5] is perhaps somewhat optimistic, but certainly these early Baptists seemed generally more aware of the need for ecclesial connections beyond the local congregation than others who followed the congregational principle. If a congregation could be recognized as a true church, then it was necessary to have the closest possible expression of unity with it. On the other hand, their theology on both sides seems to emphasize Christology as an organizing principle for ecclesiology. This certainly has its roots in the Separatist inheritance: a Separatist confession of 1596 used the threefold office of Christ, as prophet, priest and king, as a key ordering motif, and this was followed by both Helwys and the 1644 London Confession of the Particular Baptists.

The story of the Baptists had begun; their growth, however, was to be the result of the turbulent political context into which they were born. James I died in 1625 to be succeeded by his son, Charles I. Under Charles, the Church of England was led in a more Catholic direction by Archbishop William Laud and others; Charles furthered the impression that he favoured a return to Catholicism by marrying a Roman Catholic, the French princess Henrietta Maria. His relationships with his parliament deteriorated to the point where, in 1642, civil war broke out. The war was fairly even until the New Model Army was established under Sir Thomas Fairfax. The Army was a full-time, professional military organization, unlike the local militias which had preceded it; its establishment turned the war in parliament's direction. Many radical religious and political opinions were entertained and even preached within the ranks of the Army – so much so that Baptists in the Army might have looked somewhat moderate. (Politically, the Particular Baptists were often associated with the eschatologically driven radicalism of the Fifth Monarchists, while the General Baptists included several leaders who promoted the visionary socialism of the Levellers.)

When the parliamentary forces won the war, the existence and influence of the New Model Army made it impossible for parliament to impose a rigid and intolerant Presbyterian settlement, which would seem to have been its preferred option; the Army also spread Baptist (and other radical) ideas across England, and even beyond. There were Baptist congregations associated with English garrisons in both Ireland and Scotland in the 1650s. The Baptists seized the freedom given to them in the later 1640s and under the Protectorate to evangelize and plant churches; by 1660 there might have been three hundred active congregations.

They were widespread geographically, but unevenly distributed: perhaps ten congregations only in the north of England; very strong in London and the home counties, and in Somerset and Gloucestershire as a result of Thomas Collier's missionary efforts; strong in Wales after John Rede and Richard Deane commanded the army there; and strong in areas of the English midlands.

The death of Oliver Cromwell in 1658, and his son Richard's inability to fulfil his father's role, led parliament to invite King Charles's son, also called Charles, to return and restore the monarchy as the only alternative to anarchy. Charles II might have intended to reign with a measure of religious liberty – certainly he suggested so prior to his return, and he made a 'declaration of indulgence', permitting variety in worship, in 1672 – but his parliament had other ideas, and imposed a rigid and inflexible Anglican settlement, with punishment for all dissent. (The 1672 indulgence was withdrawn after just less than a year, at the insistence of parliament.) The 'Clarendon Code' – a series of acts promoting rigorous uniformity, passed 1661–5 – barred nonconformists from serving in public office or education, from meeting together for worship, or from revisiting places where that had previously ministered. Most significantly, the 1662 Act of Uniformity imposed a requirement on all clergymen to indicate by oath their acceptance of everything contained within the authorized liturgy, the *Book of Common Prayer*, and to use it alone in conducting worship.

Approximately two thousand ministers of Cromwell's state church were ejected from their posts for refusing to take the requisite oath. Most were Presbyterian in churchmanship; a significant minority were Congregationalist; only a handful were Baptist (one was Henry Jessey who, true to the principles of his old congregation, was ministering both within the state church and to a Baptist congregation). Some would later come to Baptist convictions, but the great effect of this unhappy event was to solidify English nonconformity into a major force within the nation. Had the only remaining dissenters been the little groups of Baptists, Separatists and Quakers, there would perhaps have been little pressure for toleration and little hope for survival; as it was, despite the best attempts of intolerant bishops, nonconformity was simply too strong a force to be eradicated.

However, persecution continued under Charles's reign, and in some instances increased. A revision of the Conventicles Act (forbidding gatherings for religious worship, or 'conventicles'), passed in 1670, introduced a financial incentive for people to inform on nonconformist neighbours, and removed the need for any proof before magistrates could act against a suspected illegal congregation: a conviction could be secured on the basis of 'notorious evidence and circumstance', that is, rumour. In 1679–80, parliament attempted three times to pass an act changing the royal succession to prevent the king's brother, James, who had converted to Roman Catholicism, from gaining the throne in the event of the king's death. The Protestant dissenters sided strongly with parliament on this issue; the king dissolved parliament in March 1681, and would not call another one before his death in 1685. Any sympathy he had entertained for dissenters was now gone, and most of the 1680s were desperate times of persecution for them. The General Baptist leader Francis Smith ran a newspaper which had supported the parliamentary side in the crisis; he found himself imprisoned and charged with treason; the Particular Baptist Thomas Walcott was executed for his alleged involvement in a supposed plot against the king in 1683.

The accession of James II to the throne led to an attempted Protestant rebellion, led by the Earl of Argyle and the Duke of Monmouth (an illegitimate son of Charles II). Baptists were among those rallying to the cause, and dying for it – Richard Rumboldt in Scotland with Argyle; Sampson Larke and Abraham Holmes with Monmouth in the West Country. The 'Bloody Assizes' followed, during which the Lord Chief Justice George Jeffreys repeatedly announced his desire to persecute dissenters. Later, Jeffreys would preside over the trial and execution of Elizabeth Gaunt, a Baptist who was involved in an 'underground railway', ferrying messages and people between the dissenting communities in London and the Netherlands. She was burnt alive, denied the customary mercy of strangling before the burning, at Tyburn, in October 1685. She has a minor place in history as the last woman executed for treason in Britain.

James later attempted to gain support from the dissenters by issuing two declarations of indulgence, in 1687 and 1688, but English dissent was united in welcoming the revolution of 1688 when, in a bloodless coup, parliament deposed James and bestowed the crown jointly on Mary, the eldest daughter of Charles I, and her husband, William of Orange. An Act of Toleration was soon passed which at least permitted some dissenters to worship unmolested, so long as they registered their meeting-houses with the Anglican authorities and paid taxes to support the established church. Strict limits on toleration were still in place: ministers had to sign thirty-five or thirty-six of the thirty-nine Anglican articles of religion; anti-trinitarians would not be tolerated; and all the disqualifications from public office, and from education, remained in place. Provision was at least made for those Baptists and Quakers who would not in conscience take oaths. As Underwood has it in a fine phrase '[t]he State Church was still privileged but could no longer persecute'.[6]

How strong were the two Baptist denominations at this point? Good figures are hard to come by, but we can gain some indications. In 1676, the 'Compton census' (named for the Bishop of London, Henry Compton) suggested that 4 per cent of the population of England was nonconformist; this figure is probably slightly low, and is not broken down into the different nonconformist traditions. In 1715, Presbyterian minister John Evans suggested there were 300,000 nonconformists in England and Wales, which would be about 6 per cent of the population. Of these, almost 19,000 were members or 'hearers' in 120 General Baptist congregations, whereas the Particular Baptists numbered over 40,000 in 206 congregations.[7] So the Baptists numbered about 20 per cent of the total nonconformist population, or about 1.2 per cent of the total population. For the Particular Baptists, especially, this indicates a rapid spread, given their first church was only founded in 1638 by Spilsbury.

The Eighteenth Century

In different ways, and for different reasons, much of the eighteenth century was a period of stagnation for the two denominations. The General Baptists became at the same time careless of orthodox doctrine and fixated on narrow debates about appropriate behaviour (questions such as the propriety of singing psalms in worship or the sinfulness of marrying someone who was not a member of the church preoccupied them endlessly). Many of the particular Baptists became so concerned over doctrinal orthodoxy that endless close examination of the minutiae of Calvinist doctrine occupied all their energies.

The most important of these doctrinal controversies concerned 'the modern question'. The question was whether unconverted sinners have a duty to believe in Christ. If, it was argued, some are predestined to hell, then they cannot believe; if they cannot believe, they cannot have a moral duty to believe – and if they have no duty to believe, it is inappropriate for a preacher to encourage them to believe. These ideas came into Particular Baptist life through a London minister, John Skepp, who was closely associated with John Gill, the most learned, and perhaps the most influential, minister of the mid-eighteenth century. Through the influence of Gill, and of Skepp's successor, John Brine, the Particular Baptist churches around London became places where active evangelism was regarded as a grave sin. This was not advantageous to the continued health of the denomination.

Neither Baptist tradition could remain untouched by the evangelical revival, however. Although the English strand of the revival was led by such great itinerant preachers as John Wesley and George Whitefield, their status as priests of the established church made them suspicious to English nonconformists; Isaac Watts and John Guyse's 1735 publication of Jonathan Edwards's account of the revival in Congregationalist New England was a safer introduction, at least for the Particular Baptists (Edwards, like Whitefield, was a convinced Calvinist). The Western Association of the Particular Baptists had never embraced the theology of Gill and Brine, and was fervent in its calls to prayer for a similar revival in its own life; the Yorkshire and Lancashire Association (again, Particular) benefited from several leaders who had been converted under the ministry of Whitefield and other Anglican evangelical preachers.

For a while, the influence of evangelicalism on the General Baptists was only negative. Members were lost to the 'Methodists' repeatedly, and so churches warned their remaining members not to attend evangelical meetings, on pain of discipline. However, the denomination was eventually to find new life in the revival as well. A group of evangelical societies began in the 1740s in

Leicestershire as a result of the preaching of David Taylor, servant of the Countess of Huntingdon. They formed a church in 1745, registering as Independent (i.e., Congregationalist), and soon planted other churches nearby. They came to Baptist principles in the mid-1750s, but knew no Baptist minister to receive baptism from, so two leaders baptized each other, and they became a new strand of Baptist life.

Dan Taylor, who was to become the most outstanding leader of the century among the General Baptists, was similarly a Wesleyan convert who became convinced of Baptist principles. He joined with the Lincolnshire General Baptists, and was their representative at the national assembly twice, in 1765 and 1767. However, he increasingly found the General Baptists locally and nationally to be moribund and unorthodox on important issues. He had met David Taylor's congregations, and in 1770 founded the New Connexion of General Baptists with the Leicestershire churches and other old General Baptist churches who remained orthodox and were open to evangelical practice. As the years passed, it would increase while the old General Baptist denomination decreased. What remained of the older organization became subsumed into nineteenth-century Unitarianism, eventually giving up even the practice of baptism. The continued story of the General Baptist cause was to be the story of the evangelical New Connexion.

This story, of revitalization by those coming into the denomination from the outside, was significant for the Particular Baptists as well. There is evidence to suggest that nearly two-thirds of the ministers in London in the second half of the eighteenth century had their roots outside the Baptist churches.[8] The evangelical revival even eventually penetrated those Particular Baptist churches which had embraced the theology of Gill and Brine and looked upon evangelistic preaching as a profound error. The intellectual centre of the movement shifted from London high Calvinism to an avowedly evangelical interpretation of the tradition that found its birth in the Northamptonshire Association, founded in 1764. Brine died in 1765; Gill in 1771; in 1779 Robert Hall, Snr, preached an association sermon in Northamptonshire, taking as his text Isa. 57.14: 'Prepare the way, take up the stumbling block out of the way of my people', and identifying explicitly the older theology as the block over which the movement had stumbled. The sermon was expanded and published as *Helps to Zion's Travellers* (1781). The real theological power, however, was to come from another of the Northamptonshire ministers – Andrew Fuller of Soham, and later of Kettering. Fuller found the answer to the modern question in Jonathan Edwards's distinction between 'natural' and 'moral' inability: the sinner who desired to come to Christ could come, there was no natural inability; moral inability – the lack of desire – was all that stood in the way. His *Gospel Worthy of All Acceptation* (1785) became the classic statement of evangelical Calvinism among the Baptists, and the intellectual justification for the foundation, by Fuller, William Carey and others, of the Particular Baptist Missionary Society for Propagating the Gospel among the Heathen in 1792. Carey's mission to India was the birth of the modern missionary movement, unquestionably the greatest gift that Baptists have given to the church universal.

John Rippon succeeded Gill as pastor of Carter's Lane Church in London in 1773, and remained until 1836. His services to the Particular Baptist cause were many, but among them was the publication, between 1790 and 1802, of the *Baptist Annual Register*, a periodical designed to inform Baptists about one another. It is invaluable as a source of historical material. From Rippon we learn that the New Connexion of General Baptists had 32 churches and 2,843 members in 1790; he lists the Particular Baptist churches three times, in 1790, 1794 and 1798. In part the changes are due to new information reaching Rippon, but there is also clear evidence of significant growth over the decade. Rippon does not give global membership figures, but 30,000 has been suggested for 1798.[9] According to the 1801 census, the population of England and Wales was about nine million at this point. The population had nearly doubled since Evans's estimates in 1715, but the number of Baptists had grown little. This reflects, however, significant decline through the middle of the century (Bebbington suggests as few as 16,500 Particular Baptists in 1750, and half that for the Generals[10]) and a mushrooming of growth in the later years.

What was this 'evangelical Calvinism', or 'Fullerism', theologically? Gill's argument was that, since someone predestined to be lost could not believe the gospel, it was improper to invite or command him or her to believe from the pulpit, as no-one ought to be asked to do something that is impossible for them. Furthermore, given that we cannot know who among our hearers is predestined to be lost, any sort of invitation or instruction to believe on Christ is inappropriate. The faithful pastor therefore preaches the gospel in the indicative mood, declaring what Christ has done and announcing the promises that adhere to all who believe; the imperative mood ('Put your faith in Jesus! Save yourself!') must be avoided.

To combat this, Fuller borrowed a distinction from Jonathan Edwards's *Freedom of the Will*, between 'moral' and 'natural' inability. There are some things I cannot do because of realities of nature that are simply beyond my control: I cannot fly; I cannot lift a tonne of weight; I cannot supply sufficient aid to alleviate a widespread natural disaster. These are 'natural' inabilities in Edwards's (and Fuller's) terms. However, other inabilities are of another sort: the drunkard, unable to resist finishing the bottle; a serial philanderer, giving in again to the same old temptation. Edwards's insight was that these are not instances of some special psychological category such as addiction, but the normal stuff of human life. Many of our decisions are dictated by who we are, and we are unable not to be who we are. This creates another form of inability, 'moral' inability. For Edwards, the point of all this was ethical: suppose I see a drowning child whom I fail to help; am I at fault? Not if my failure was due to an inability to swim ('natural' inability); but if my failure was due to moral inability, an inability to care, then the answer would be yes.

Fuller's point is a development of this. This distinction, he sees, is an answer to Gill's logic. The sinner who is unable to respond to the gospel because he or she is too in love with his or her sin is prevented by a moral inability, not a natural one. It is appropriate, then, to call, and even to implore and persuade, the sinner to repent. Perhaps, by the grace of God, our efforts will become the means (under God) by which the sinners see the truth of their condition, and has their heart changed. Moral suasion is appropriate in the face of moral inability, as addressing, and potentially removing, the source of the inability. Moral suasion, of course, is an inappropriate and ineffectual means of combating natural inability.

By 1800, the British Baptist movement was beginning to find a new strength. It was still divided between Arminian and

Calvinist strands, but both were finding new life in the evangelical movement. The Christological emphasis and connexionalism that marked the earliest days were both still strong. While the Anglican and Presbyterian churches had begun to be changed by a new, 'liberal', theology which was doubtful that the claims of the Bible might be straightforwardly true, such ideas had little purchase among Baptists, except the older General Baptists, who were drifting rapidly into numerical and theological irrelevance. There had, however, been a parallel – although somewhat different – development of Baptist life across the Atlantic, and it is to this I now turn.

Chapter 2
Baptists in North America

Beginnings

Although the Pilgrim Fathers were closely related ecclesially to the founders of the Baptist movement, Smyth and Helwys, there is no evidence that any of them accepted Baptist principles. Their celebrated journey westward in search of freedom to practice the religion they believed the Bible to teach is, however, illustrative of a much more general move. It is no surprise either that some who entertained doubts over the practice of infant baptism should be a part of this migration, or that some who had travelled over should later come to something resembling a Baptist position in their ongoing quest for true, New Testament, Christianity.

Baptist life in North America can be traced back to the 1630s, at least, with two churches being formed in that decade in Rhode Island. Ezekiel Holliman, Roger Williams (who I discuss at some length in Chapter 6 below) and others formed a Baptist congregation at Providence in 1638, and John Clarke started a church at Newport in 1639–40. Both suffered disagreements and splits, the Providence church gradually identifying with a stream of the English General Baptists, and the Newport congregation splitting in 1671, with a group embracing 'Seventh day' principles (worship and Sabbath observance should be on Saturday, not Sunday) founding a new congregation. The first congregation to cross the Atlantic together would seem to be one pastored by John Myles, who moved his people from Ilston in Wales to Rehoboth in Massachusetts in 1663. The churches split, or sought to plant other congregations. or split; more Baptists came across the Atlantic, and by 1700 Baptist life in the American colonies was reasonably extensive and varied.

In 1707 the first Association was formed, centred on Philadelphia, composed of five congregations of Calvinistic Baptists in the Delaware River Valley. The settlement of Philadelphia had been founded in 1681 by William Penn, a Quaker, and offered a context of religious tolerance unlike that found in New England. (To illustrate the intolerance of the more northern colonies, Henry Dunster had been removed from his position as president of Harvard when, in 1652, he refused to have his child baptized; Thomas Goold, who founded the first Baptist church in Boston in 1663 was repeatedly fined and intermittently imprisoned for his beliefs; Massachussetts passed a law in 1728, reaffirmed several times throughout the eighteenth century, that required Baptist and Quaker churches to be registered by the Congregationalist establishment.) The Philadelphia Association adopted the Second London Confession of Faith, the 1677 Baptistic revision of the Westminster Confession, as its basis of faith in 1742, and published Benjamin Griffith's *The Power and Duty of an Association of Churches* in 1746. These two documents became pivotal for the developing Baptist traditions in North America. The Philadelphia Association was also involved in the founding of a Baptist college in Rhode Island in 1764 (now Brown University, and no longer with any Baptist affiliation). The principle of association with other true churches was as important for the American Baptists as for their British cousins.

Around the time the college was being founded in Rhode Island, Ebenezer Moulton was founding the first Baptist church in what is now Canada, at a settlement called Mud Flats (later Horton Landing). Moulton was a merchant who had prospered in Massachusetts during the French and Indian War (1756–63); after the war ended, however, his business collapsed, and he joined the thousands of settlers who accepted the British government's invitation to move from New England to settle the previously French-held lands to the north. In the last decade of the eighteenth century, several Baptist congregations were planted in Canada by missionaries sent from Vermont to Quebec, and from New York to the shores of Lake Ontario.

Like their co-religionists in England, Baptists in America were to gain new vigour through people of other religious traditions who were influenced by the Great Awakening (the parallel movement to the British evangelical revival), and then found their way to

Baptistic convictions. A particular feature of the Awakening was concern over practices such as the 'half-way covenant' that had grown up among the Congregational churches of New England. This was an accommodation that allowed those who could not profess experience of a saving conversion to nonetheless enjoy at least some of the benefits of church membership. It was necessary because church membership was a requirement for full participation in civil society in many of the colonies at the time.

Awakened firebrands such as James Davenport were profoundly critical of the sleepy state of the churches they saw, often denouncing ministers as strangers to the gospel. Under such preaching, it is perhaps not surprising that a pressure to create 'Separate' churches, which maintained a purity of doctrine and a fully converted membership, should arise. As had happened among the English Separatists a century before, once questions of the legitimacy of the historic churches were on the agenda, many became convinced of the wrongness of the baptism of infants – this was a practice, after all, which seemed routinely to confer some measure of church membership on those who, most of all, could not confess their saving faith.

The most famous person to walk this route was undoubtedly Isaac Backus. Backus was converted under Davenport's preaching in 1741, and was part of the founding of a Separate church a few years later. In 1748, he was called as minister of a new Separate congregation in Middleborough, Massachusetts. There, he became convinced of the rightness of restricting baptism to believers alone. He was baptized in 1751, but remained for a while pastor of the Separate church. Eventually, he formed a new, Baptist, congregation in Middleborough in 1756. Backus became a leading statesman among the Baptists and, in 1774, was entrusted with carrying a petition pleading for religious liberty to the Continental Congress. In 1777, he published a famous letter to the citizens of New England, pleading for the cause of religious liberty. After the war, he made an astonishing three thousand-mile tour of the Baptist causes, preaching and helping where he could, and collecting materials for his *History of New England with particular reference to the people called Baptists* (1804). I will say more about Backus's campaigns for liberty of conscience in Chapter 6 below.

The Congregationalists had come to the colonies wanting freedom to practise their own religion, not wanting freedom for all to practise religion. Those Congregationalists ('Independents') who remained behind in old England, under successive Anglican and Presbyterian regimes, had made common cause with Baptists and Quakers in demanding freedom of belief for all. In New England and the other colonies, by contrast, the call that all should be free to follow God as their consciences dictated, and the conviction that it was wrong to be forced to pay taxes to support a ministry they believed to be false, became a Baptist distinctive, shared only with the Quakers. It was this cause, against the Massachusetts Standing Order, among other such laws, that Backus was sent to champion. After the War of Independence, the separation of church and state was enshrined in (the first amendment to) the Constitution of the new republic, but it would be 1833 before Baptists gained the freedom to worship without penalty or restriction that this seemed to promise in every state.

Baptists served with distinction in the War of Independence, and generally supported the cause. There are, however, some instances – Morgan Edwards of Philadelphia being the most notable – of Baptist leaders who declared Loyalist sympathies. More interestingly, perhaps, was the stance of the German Baptist community which had travelled to enjoy the liberty of religious freedom in Pennsylvania, settling west of Philadelphia, initially around Wissahickon, and then moving to Ephrata. They remained aloof from the war, refusing to support any army out of religious principle. For their stance, they were fined by the colonial government.

The Nineteenth Century

There is no doubt that the great story of American Baptists during the nineteenth century is one of growth. A movement that numbered perhaps 100,000 adherents in 1800 could claim three million in 1900 – although the majority of this growth was in the second half of the century (in 1850 the Baptists were just over 300,000 strong). The main institutional motor for this growth was the local revival, a time when a heightened religious interest seemed to pervade a whole community, and regular, perhaps daily, meetings would be held, at which spontaneous manifestations of religious fervour or concern, such as weeping and shouting, would take place. Meetings like this were particularly important on the frontier, where congregations were often very small, and any form of settled ministry uncommon.

Such revivals – complete with similarly spectacular manifestations – reach back, of course, to the beginnings of the Great Awakening under the ministry of Jonathan Edwards in Northampton in 1734–5 (and indeed deeper, back into regular colonial Puritan experience); Edwards had fought hard at the time against both those (like Davenport, under whose preaching Backus was converted) who thought that such manifestations were incontrovertible evidence that God was at work and those who thought that they were signs of disorder, inappropriate for a Christian meeting. For Edwards, the ecstatic manifestations of revival proved nothing: someone deeply affected by a saving work of the Spirit might well cry out in such a manner; but so might someone merely caught up in the excitement and emotion of the moment.[1] In the nineteenth century, what might be called a 'science of revival' began to develop: recognizing that the emotional context of the revival meeting unquestionably led to responses, revivalists investigated the use of 'means' to heighten the emotional context, and so to increase the number of responses. The great name in this endeavour is Charles Finney, a Presbyterian, but Finney's 'New Measures' were eagerly adopted by many Baptists.

Theologically speaking, what is going on here? It is fair to say that Finney, still more his followers, were somewhat impatient of theological questions, being more interested in what worked. We can tell this story theologically, however, if we are prepared to borrow the narratives of the English Baptists from a generation before. Hall, Fuller, Carey and others, found their liberation in a Calvinism that proposed that there was a role for human action, particularly moral suasion, in the working out of God's decrees; the 'New Measures' took this understanding to a new level, suggesting that every humanly available psychological influence or measure should be deployed to entice people to place their faith in Christ. If language, or music, or decor, or anything else, can be manipulated to encourage people to respond positively to the gospel offer, then in every case the manipulation should be performed; in every case it is a part of God's sovereign action in bringing people to faith.

This missionary energy was harnessed in the founding of a multitude of mission organizations, beginning with the New York Missionary Society, founded on 21 September 1796, with the aim of converting the Native Americans. Other societies focused on the African-Americans in the South, the frontiersmen and on overseas mission. These societies became the focus of perhaps the most protracted disagreement among American Baptists in the nineteenth century, the antimission controversy. The 'Black Rock Address',[2] agreed by a meeting of delegates of churches in Baltimore in 1832, is a classic statement of the anti-mission, or 'Old School' (the term used in the opening line of the address) position: on the basis of an insistence on direct Scriptural justification for all practices, tract societies, Sunday schools, the American Bible Society, mission societies, theological colleges and protracted mission meetings, are each assessed and found wanting. The rhetoric is direct and often withering (of 'Theological Schools': 'in every age, from the school of Alexandria down to this day, they have been a real pest to the church of Christ'; of 'the modern missionary': '[h] is leading motive, judging from his movements, is not love to souls, but love of fame'). The theological basis of such rejection is clear: a hard line is repeatedly drawn between divine saving action and appointed means, and any human attempt to create conditions conducive to response. There were also less theological reasons for opposition to missions evident, however, notably a concern over the constant appeals for funds, and a distrust of power being concentrated into the hands of boards and presidents.

Theologically, the anti-mission movement, and the Primitive Baptist position it gave rise to, was a continuation of the high Calvinism of Gill and Brine. The language of 'duty faith' (i.e., that it is a duty of all people to believe the gospel), so central to the 'modern question' that preoccupied English Baptists in the seventeenth century, was being used in debates among some American Baptists as late as 1887.[3] The debate over the use of 'means' can be read as another manifestation of the same theological point, in that it is also about the relation of divine sovereignty and human activity. For the missionary Baptists, following Fuller, God worked sovereignly through human actions to change minds and hearts; for the Primitives, other than certain specially appointed means (notably doctrinal preaching), God's working of salvation had to be separated from any human activity. The debate over biblical authority turned on the extensiveness of revelation: does Scripture intend to exclude anything it does not mention, or only those things specifically forbidden? Missionary Baptists assumed the latter: there is liberty to employ any practice not explicitly forbidden in Scripture. The Primitive position is similar to the (much more carefully stated) 'Regulative principle' adopted by certain Presbyterian churches, that in Christian worship, only those things commanded or recorded in Scripture are appropriate.

The Primitive Baptist movement spread rapidly; before 1850, there were already 1,600 congregations and 60,000 members.[4] A small Freewill (i.e., Arminian) Primitive Baptist movement began in Canada in 1875 on the same grounds, but dwindled away over the following decades. The US Primitives remain in existence in various guises, with something like 2,200 churches and a membership of over 100,000.[5] They (mostly) take the 1677 Second London Confession as their doctrinal standard. (In the American context this is often known as the '1689 Confession'; it was written in 1677, but approved by the Particular Baptist Assembly in 1689.)

Other disagreements and splits occurred in the Baptist movement throughout the nineteenth century. From a theological perspective, one of the stranger divisions was the rise of Landmarkism. Taking its name from a pamphlet published by James M. Pendleton in 1854, 'An Old Landmark Re-set', Landmarkism reflected a vision of Baptist life as radically different from any other tradition of Christianity, every other tradition being judged apostate. Any form of ecumenical cooperation was therefore excluded – the 'gospel' preached by a Methodist minister is no gospel at all, and one professing conversion on hearing such a sermon remains deluded in darkness and sin. This principle was applied diachronically as well as synchronically, and so Landmarkism posited a pure succession of churches and ministers, linking the (Baptist) churches of today to the time of the apostles. The crucial mark of this succession was the rite of baptism, which must, to be valid, be performed by a minister commissioned by a true Baptist church. Just as early nineteenth-century Anglo-Catholicism staked its legitimacy on a (highly dubious) claim of an unbroken succession of episcopal ordination, so Landmark Baptists hazarded their claim to be the true church on a (profoundly implausible) assertion of an unbroken succession of baptismal immersion. The strength of this strange position can be seen in the unfortunate fate of William T. Whitsitt, a capable historian who was forced to resign as president of the Southern Baptist Theological Seminary after mentioning (correctly) in an encyclopaedia article that Baptists first adopted immersion as the mode of baptism around 1641.

Other divisions ran along ethnic lines. The mass immigration from continental Europe to America during the century resulted in significant communities eager to maintain their own ethnic/cultural identity in the new land. Some of the immigrants were already Baptist, fruits of Oncken's astonishing labours (see next chapter); others were targeted by Baptist evangelists. Missionary outreach to these communities was no doubt intended to integrate them into the mainstream of the denomination, but the result was in fact the founding variously of the German Baptist Conference (1851), the Rock Island Conference of Swedish Baptists (1856) and the Danish-Norwegian Conference (1883).

Unquestionably the most significant structural split in the nineteenth century, however, was regional, with the establishment of the Southern Baptist Convention (SBC) in 1845, bringing an end to the national representative function of the Triennial Convention. (There had been earlier splits in smaller Baptist bodies, notably the Freewill Baptist General Conference breaking fellowship with churches in the Carolinas over slavery in 1839.) The SBC was organized along different lines to the old convention, and tensions over organizational patterns certainly played their part in the split. The crucial issue, however, was slavery. In the main, the debate over slavery was remarkably untheologized. In the 1840s, the national Baptist organizations generally attempted to avoid or ignore the issue. The (in)famous 'Baltimore Compromise' of the General Missionary Convention (GMC) asserted in 1840 that the GMC took no position on the issue of slavery; four years later this was reaffirmed, the Convention 'disclaiming all sanction of slavery or antislavery'.[6] The issue could not be ducked, however: already in 1831, Nat Turner, a black Baptist lay preacher, had been executed after leading a slave revolt in Virginia; and in the mid-1840s, the state Convention of Georgia tested national organizations by proposing well-known slave owners as potential missionaries. Meanwhile, in the North, a minority, at least, of Baptists were coming to the view, already common in Europe, that slaveholding and Christian discipleship were incompatible. The Southern associations pointed to the undeniable fact that slave-holding was known and not condemned by the New Testament writers.

The attitude that there is something intrinsically superior about people of Anglo-Saxon stock persisted in (Southern) Baptist rhetoric, even in the most official pronouncements, right through the nineteenth century, and justified Baptist support for, and involvement in, the segregationist policies[7] that were put in place after defeat in the Civil War forced abolition on the Southern states. Prior to the war, Baptist churches in the South had not been segregated; indeed, slaves were allowed most of the privileges and responsibilities of membership (generally they were not permitted a vote in church meetings), were accorded the same title of 'sister' or 'brother' as white church members and could teach Sunday School or serve as deacons. There was no willingness to extend such partial and limited expressions of equality following emancipation, however, and the result was an exodus of black Baptists from the old churches and associations. Generally, this was accepted as inevitable, and perhaps even desirable, on both sides, and the process was astonishingly rapid. Baptist life in the old South was virtually completely segregated within a decade of emancipation in 1865.

Initially, these huge organizational splits, of South from North, and on racial lines in the South, had little visible impact on Baptist theology. This is perhaps unsurprising; the issues behind the splits were not primarily theological, and so the new bodies that were formed created the context in which theological views might diverge in the future, rather than concretizing existing divisions. That said, a surprising degree of theological unity remained within the US Baptist movement through the nineteenth century; intellectual divisions lagged behind organizational divisions by some decades.

Modernism and Fundamentalism

The second half of the nineteenth century was marked, theologically, by increased openness to the new 'liberal' theologies coming out of Germany. Three streams of thought came together to form the new theology of the day. First was an emphasis on religious experience after the manner of Schleiermacher. This was particularly enticing to evangelical Baptists raised in the revivalist tradition: it is not a large step from demanding evidence of truly gracious experience from the claimed convert prior to baptism and membership to assuming that experience is the crucial validation of all theological themes. Schleiermacher's programme, it should be remembered, was profoundly apologetic; the turn to experience was a way of demonstrating the continued relevance of Christianity when older, more rationalistic, proofs seemed to have failed. A convincing apologetic coupled with a stress on experiential religion was an enticing mixture for Baptists. Second was a belief concerning the centrality of history. In the German tradition, this was the inheritance of Hegel, who believed in an immanent and inevitable historical progress towards perfection; later in the century, it chimed perfectly with the post-Darwinian fad of applying the concept of evolution to everything, not just the origin of species. Mid-nineteenth-century American Baptists, heirs to the post-millennial hopes of Edwards and his followers, and surrounded by the language of 'manifest destiny' could find this, too, an attractive intellectual option. The result, however, could be a privileging of contemporary intellectual fashions over the settled faith of the church which, insensitively handled (as it was by Foster of Chicago, as we shall see) could be incendiary. The third aspect of the new theology to be mentioned is a stress on the ethical content of the faith as more important than the dogmatic. In Germany, Ritschl or von Harnack spring to mind; for the Baptist preacher in America, struggling with an astonishing rate of cultural change, and challenges to faith from science and from biblical criticism, to be able to point to the ethical character of Jesus and take a stand on its wonder and the perfection must have been enormously attractive.

The seeds were sown in the first half of the century: Irah Chase, who had taught in Philadelphia, was in Germany listening to lectures in several different universities in 1823, and soon after his return was to become president of the new Newton Theological Institute, where he modelled the curriculum on his German experience, with a particular focus on higher criticism. At Colgate, the first president, Nathaniel Kendrick (elected in 1836), fused his own revivalist background with Schleiermachian themes to develop a theology based on, or at least ratified by, religious experience. At Rochester, Ezekiel G. Robinson sought a mediating theology, not heterodox, but dismissive of the attitude of those such as the Old Princetonians who (in his view) tried to ignore the great advances in theological science the century had brought; his student and successor Augustus H. Strong followed a similar path for the forty years of his professorship, becoming perhaps the most respected Baptist theologian of his day.

Strong was one of a number of powerful voices advocating, or at least modelling, a cautious openness to the new theology among Baptists at the turn of the century. His personal standing, and long tenure as president of Rochester (1862–1912), made his views respectable, even when challenging. The same could be said of other contemporary long-serving seminary presidents: Alvah Hovey, president of Newton 1868–98; Henry Weston, president of Crozer 1868–1908; and Edgar Y. Mullins, president of the Southern Baptist Seminary 1899–1928. Each of these men led their institutions in engaging with (even when not completely accepting of) biblical criticism and liberal theology; each of them had the personal credibility with their constituency to allow this engagement to be acceptable.

If Strong was the most able theologian of the group, the most significant thinker for the development of Baptist life was unquestionably Mullins. Mullins's theology might also be described as mediating; he displayed early in his tenure a fine political instinct in being able both to retain good relations with the locally strong Landmarkian constituency and to maintain scholarly credibility with the northern schools. If some of his theological work appears as little more than the careful expression of this fine political balance, he gradually developed a distinctive vision of Baptist beliefs, centred upon his enormously influential idea of soul competency (for more on this see Chapter 6), and the concomitant commitment to human rights, particularly religious liberty. Towards the end of his life this perhaps lost him some of his more conservative friends in the South, but it propelled him to worldwide prominence in the Baptist movement. He became president of the Baptist World Alliance in 1928.

Alongside these four leaders, the organization of the (Baptist-funded) University of Chicago in the 1890s led to the creation of the famous and influential 'Chicago School' of theology, developed by such thinkers as G. W. Northrup, Shirley Jackson Chase and William R. Harper, the first president of the university. At the heart of this new approach to theology was an insistence on the historical contingency and development of theological ideas (the so-called 'genetic method'). History and context would be studied to understand how beliefs had grown, changed and developed. Characteristically for the day, it was assumed that historical change would be in the form of an evolution, a move from primitive to more sophisticated forms (a view of theology already evident in Schleiermacher's classification scheme for different religious expressions, of course). For the first half of the twentieth century, almost every Baptist seminary in the US and Canada would have one or more faculty trained in this tradition; the influence also spread widely beyond the Baptists and beyond the North American continent.

What were the practical results of this openness to more 'liberal' traditions of theology? We might point to changed language in defining and proclaiming the gospel: a proclamation of forgiveness for guilty rebels deserving of condemnation was replaced by a gentler, if no less insistent, call to embrace and align oneself with the love of God and the extension of the Kingdom on earth. The most sustained and eloquent expression of this last point, was undoubtedly the 'social gospel' developed (among the Baptists) by Walter Rauschenbusch, sometime pastor in the German Baptist Conference of America in 'Hell's Kitchen', New York, and later holder of a chair in Rochester. Believing in the power of human agency to bring about real social change, and the pressing ethical demands of the gospel, those influenced by the social gospel worked tirelessly, and often very effectively, in the cause of labour rights, the better treatment of immigrants and international justice through the early decades of the twentieth century. Rauschenbusch's influence can be seen even half a century later in the theology of the civil rights movement (Martin Luther King Jr, for example, described the 'indelible influence' that reading Rauschebusch left on him).

Unlike the British evangelical social reformers of a century before (see next chapter), or Finney and those who followed him in linking the revivalist campaigns of the 1830s with the abolitionist cause, however, the proponents of the social gospel tended to divorce their concern for justice from personal evangelism. A reaction was inevitable – indeed, already brewing in Bible Conferences up and down the land. It came to profound public notice, however, in the second decade of the new century, as a result of two Presbyterian laymen becoming aware of an internal Baptist dispute, centred on the Chicago School.

One of Harper's earliest intentions as president of Chicago was to lure the Baptist theologian George B. Foster out of McMaster University in Toronto. It took him four years to succeed, but in 1896 Foster took a position in Chicago. Foster took the genetic views of his new home to an extreme, combining them with a Schleiermachian stress on religious experience and a typically liberal concern for ethics. For him, the essence of Christianity was the moral perfection of Jesus of Nazareth, and the heartfelt response this engendered in the one who sought to follow after Jesus. Doctrines – including the deity of Christ, and even basic theism – were expressions of changing and developing human responses to this essence, and the need for theology as the century turned was to complete the task of restating this unchanging essence in doctrines suited for the new age. In 1906, he published *The Finality of the Christian Religion*, stating these ideas clearly and rousing the ire of A. C. Dixon, recently arrived as pastor of Moody Memorial Church, and a veteran of early proto-fundamentalist controversies.[8] Dixon began to speak against 'Fosterism', expressing himself as particularly scandalized that someone holding such views could draw a 'Baptist salary'.

In one such attack, delivered in 1909 in Los Angeles, Dixon was heard by Lyman Stewart, a lay Presbyterian, millionaire and oil magnate. Stewart was impressed enough to share with Dixon a plan he had to publish pamphlets defending historic Christian truth, and to send them to every pastor and church worker in the nation. Milton Stewart, his brother, agreed to help finance the operation; Dixon agreed to serve as editor, and *The Fundamentals* was born. The series ran from 1910 to 1915, and eventually included ninety separate essays in twelve volumes.[9] Dixon edited the first five; R. A. Torrey the latter seven. Dixon was a long-time admirer of the great English Baptist preacher, C. H. Spurgeon (indeed, he served as pastor of Spurgeon's church, the Metropolitan Tabernacle in London, 1911–19), and sought in various ways to evoke the spirit of the Down Grade Controversy (for more on which see next chapter) in his editorship of *The Fundamentals*. Spurgeon's son, Thomas, was asked to contribute a chapter, on 'Salvation by Grace', as was T. W. Medhurst, Spurgeon's first student at the Pastor's College (who wrote on 'Is Romanism Christianity?').

The term 'fundamentalism' later acquired a strong implication of anti-intellectualism; this should not be read back into these original publications, which featured an impressive array of leading figures, some by no means anti-intellectual or ultra-conservative.[10] Even such later shibboleths as the historicity of the early chapters of Genesis were openly doubted within the essays.[11] With hindsight, the fundamentalist movement was already bifurcating, perhaps especially among Baptists, and Dixon was visibly on the moderate wing. The most high profile of the militants was W. B. Riley of Minnesota, who was also the driving force behind the World Christian Fundamentals Association (WCFA, founded 1919). Throughout the early 1920s, Riley bombarded the Northern Convention with demands that strict confessional tests be instituted for ministers, missionaries and college teachers. The Convention was steadfast in its refusal. In hindsight, the decisive point in the battle, although by no means the last engagement, was the reaffirmation at the 1922 NBC annual meeting that the New Testament alone was the basis of belief and practice. Riley was instrumental in organizing the Baptist Bible Union (BBU) in 1923 and, after the BBU's effective collapse in 1930, he was involved in the formation in 1932 of the General Association of Regular Baptist Churches (GARBC), although Robert Ketcham became the key leader within this.

The moderate fundamentalists were distinguished from the militants more by tactics than belief in the early stages of the movement. Rather than confrontational demands, they sought change through influencing Convention structures, and particularly through the hope that newly founded conservative seminaries might raise up a new generation of orthodox ministers. The effect of the new seminaries, however, was often polarizing, particularly as they tended to be founded in the same cities as older training institutions (Northern Baptist Theological Seminary opened alongside the university in Chicago in 1913; Eastern Baptist in Philadelphia, the same city as Crozer; the Boston Missionary Training School, founded by A. J. Gordon in 1889, was undenominational, but [as Gordon College] became a centre for evangelical ministerial formation rivalling Newton). In 1946, seeing the failure of their tactics, many of the moderate fundamentalists also split from the NBC to form the Conservative Baptist Fellowship.

In the South, a similar pattern of denominational division can be seen, coupled with a renewed Landmarkism. The latter was agitated for particularly by B. M. Bogard, who used his editorship of the *Arkansas Baptist* from 1904 on to oppose the 'episcopal' tendencies he saw in the SBC, while leading breakaway Landmarkist organizations, first in Arkansas, and then nationally. This culminated in the fundamentalist and Landmarkist American Baptist Missionary Association, founded in 1924. Non Landmarkist Southern Baptist fundamentalism found its most high-profile leader in J. Franklyn ('Frank') Norris, who was involved in the founding of the WCFA and the BBU. Similarly to Riley in the North, Norris first attempted an aggressive reform campaign within his denomination, and then rapidly left, founding the Premillennial Baptist Missionary Fellowship (later the World Baptist Fellowship [WBF]) in 1933–4. (Jerry Falwell's Liberty Baptist Fellowship traces its origins to the WBF.)

Similar stories can be told of Canada: Toronto Baptist Seminary opened as a rival to McMaster in 1927; again, in the same year, the Regular Baptist Churches of British Colombia were organized as a new denomination after a failed attempt to impose confessional standards on the BC Baptist Convention. The fundamentalist wing of Canadian Baptist life has been less fissiparous than the US equivalents, and in 1953 most of the major groups in fact merged to form the Fellowship of evangelical Baptist Churches in Canada.

What were the doctrinal issues at stake? Fundamentalism was initially a reactionary movement, united more in its opposition to new theological trends than by its commitment to positive proposals of its own. It took its stand on: the inerrancy of Scripture, and with it the veracity of biblical reports of the virgin birth; the miracles of Christ, and the Resurrection; the depravity of all human people; the substitutionary atonement of Christ, and the damnation to eternal conscious torment of the unsaved; the visible return of Christ, often with a commitment to a pre-millennial, pre-tribulational eschatological scheme. There is not much in this list, however, that many Baptists (or indeed other evangelicals) could not affirm. This has led many commentators to suggest that fundamentalism is not to be understood as a distinctive theological movement, but as a culture, or a sociological phenomenon. Memorably, George Marsden defined a fundamentalist as 'an evangelical who is angry about something'.[12]

This suggests that the essence of fundamentalism is not the holding of particular doctrines, but a particular posture and attitude towards the wider world. The precise attitude that has characterized the fundamentalist subculture among American protestants, including Baptists, is perhaps less anger than fear. After the public relations disaster of the Scopes trial in 1925, American fundamentalism became an extraordinarily insular movement, focusing on the creation of counter-cultural church communities and parallel educational institutions. A generation later, fundamentalist media outlets developed, particularly in the broadcast media. Fundamentalism became a subculture that shunned any contact with the wider world, apparently because of fear of contamination.

For this reason, many of the visible groups described as 'fundamentalist' in recent decades perhaps represent a departure from the traditions of the movement, or at least a new stage of expression of it. Pat Robertson, a former Southern Baptist, unquestionably has roots in fundamentalism, but his repeated willingness to seek to engage with the secular political process is at odds with the movement as it developed in the 1930s; equally, to describe those responsible for the conservative realignment of the SBC in the 1980s (on which see below) as 'fundamentalists' seems to miss the point rather completely: they succeeded in reshaping their denomination, where Norris and Riley had failed, and so they had no need to follow Norris and Riley in withdrawing into a fundamentalist ghetto. The emergence of a confident movement, conservative in theology and politics, and aggressively engaged in pressing its agendas on denominational and political structures alike, is something new; related no doubt theologically – and indeed in terms of institutions and individuals – to the older fundamentalism, but not identical with it.

The emergence of this movement is perhaps the most significant event for a theological history of Baptists in America in the twentieth century. Through the middle years of the century there were hot divisions within the churches, as within the broader society, on the major cultural disagreements. To take only the most obvious example, while the most high-profile leader of the civil rights movement, Martin Luther King, Jr, was a Baptist pastor, drawing inspiration from Baptist sources – notably Rauschenbusch – as well as broader Christian (Niebuhr) and non-Christian (Gandhi) traditions, many Baptists were implacably opposed: James McClendon (who I will consider in more detail in Chapter 4) was removed from his faculty position at a Baptist seminary because of his vocal support for civil rights, for example. That said, the public face of Baptist life in North America was theologically moderate, ecumenically engaged and often socially liberal. Since the 1970s, however, there has been a resurgence of a much more conservative tradition, fully publicly engaged.

The beginnings of this resurgence can be traced to the 1950s, and the birth of the new evangelicalism in the US. Individuals (most notably the Baptist Billy Graham); organizations, such as the newly founded National Association of Evangelicals; educational institutions, such as Fuller; and media outlets, such as *Christianity Today*, all committed to a new combination of evangelical doctrinal orthodoxy and committed public engagement. If Billy Graham was the most visible and effective Baptist proponent of this new mood, its most able theologian was another Baptist, Carl F. Henry. Whatever may be thought of Henry's great work *God, Revelation and Authority* in purely academic terms today, its significance cannot be overstated in the way it called American evangelicals back to the task of serious theological scholarship that took on the wider academic world, rather than ignoring it, or dismissing it as 'secular' and so unworthy of engagement.

This resurgence has been wider than just Baptist: indeed, many of its most characteristic manifestations are undenominational (for example, the Moral Majority and later manifestations of the religious right) or deliberately organized across denominations (for example, such recent groups as Together for the Gospel, or the Gospel Coalition). That said, there is significant Baptist involvement in many of these organizations, and it might be that the realignment of the Southern Baptist Convention represents this movement's most complete success to date. Paul Pressler III, a Baptist layman and judge, became concerned that students in Baylor University were losing their conviction of the truth of the Bible as a result of their studies. In 1978 he met with Paige Patterson and together they planned how to halt the march of liberalizing tendencies within the denomination. Patterson was already a respected conservative theologian; Pressler's legal training gave him a particular awareness of how power was distributed in organizations, and he perceived how the policies of the SBC could be decisively affected simply by influencing a few key appointments. (Essentially, the situation was not unlike that of the Supreme Court in Washington, DC: the president of the Convention could not influence policies directly, but had the power to decide on appointments to the committees which could; by ensuring a relatively brief series of like-minded presidents, a working majority could be gained on all the key committees.)

Pressler and Patterson initially worked simply to ensure that all Convention staff were committed to biblical inerrancy; in a sense, therefore, their doctrinal programme was minimalist. That said, on the one hand, a commitment to inerrancy was so closely bound up with other doctrinal positions that, in practice, this ensured a certain theological narrowness; on the other, there has been a recent tradition in the SBC of identifying certain shibboleths that would serve as proxy test cases for a real commitment to biblical inerrancy, the two most famous being a cessationist position on concerning supernatural spiritual gifts and a commitment to male headship in (at least) family and church. By insisting that one is clearly not truly committed to inerrancy unless one holds to such positions (a claim that, as a student of the history of evangelical theology, appears to me to be very difficult to justify), one makes the apparently minimalist doctrinal bar of inerrancy an open-ended doctrinal test which could potentially be used to impose an astonishingly narrow theological programme. (Consider, by contrast, the equally serious commitment to inerrancy as the membership standard for the (American) Evangelical Theological Society: the ETS has repeatedly judged that, because biblical interpretation is not a finished task, an extraordinarily wide variety of positions may be compatible with a commitment to biblical inerrancy, and so may be held in good conscience by its members.)

Pressler, Patterson and their supporters, would claim that they were acting to prevent Convention staff from espousing positions, that were in fact unrepresentative of the generality of Southern Baptists. This claim must be taken seriously: there is considerable data to show that denominational staffers are, on average, significantly less traditionally orthodox than ministers in pastoral charge on a whole range of issues across all major American denominations. From a Baptist perspective, if genuine power is invested in denominational staff – and some of the key targets within the SBC were those who appointed teaching faculty to seminaries, and those who approved mission expenditure – then it is entirely appropriate for a grass-roots movement to attempt to force denominational staff to be more representative of the generality of the membership of the denomination. (I will discuss the reaction over the perception of Christological unorthodoxy on the part of a speaker at the Baptist Union of Great Britain annual assembly in the next chapter; it was less well-organized and less long-lasting than the work of Pressler and Patterson, but it similarly represented as an attempt to call denominational leadership into line with the views of the local membership.)

That said, what is appropriate for Baptists is that the denominational structures represent the grass-roots, not that they become unrepresentative in the opposite direction in some sort of 'pendulum swing' move. The SBC in 1978 had a significant moderate wing, which probably was over-represented in the central structures; in not very many years, the moderates came to believe that they were essentially excluded from central structures, and a series of significant breakaways followed: the Alliance of

Baptists in 1987, the Cooperative Baptist Fellowship in 1991 and the Mainstream Baptist Network in 1997. Strikingly, when the SBC chose to disaffiliate from the World Baptist Alliance in 2004, a decision presented as a marker of a simply different vision of what it is to be Baptist, many of the State Conventions immediately reaffiliated in their own right, suggesting that the present leadership of the SBC is at least as unrepresentative of its constituent churches as the leadership that Pressler objected to in the 1970s. (The point here is not the theological correctness of one side or the other: for Baptists, the local church is the place where, uniquely, Christ's mind is known; on this basis, the only legitimacy a Baptist denominational leadership can have is in representing the views of the local churches they are called to serve; when it ceases to do this and starts pursuing a political agenda not mandated by the several church meetings to which it is called to be responsible, in Baptist terms, at least, it has ceased to be legitimate – and this judgement must be made, even by someone in profound sympathy with the agenda pursued.)

At the time of writing, it is fair to say that the Southern Baptist Convention remains intent, as an organization, on separating itself from the wider Baptist world (and indeed almost anybody else) and claiming, with all the energy and conviction that Helwys once displayed in making the same claim, that it alone understands and practises authentic Christianity. That said, the scholar does not need to do extensive fieldwork to discover that this monolithic self-presentation of the denominational bureaucracy is hardly representative of the generality of Southern Baptists. A theological turn to a more self-consciously Calvinistic theology has led some leaders to make broad and extensive common cause with theologically conservative but non-Baptist leaders and groups, such as the Presbyterian Church of America; when one considers that leaders of the stature of Mark Dever and, particularly, Al Mohler are so engaged, this can hardly be dismissed as a minor aberration. Equally, a disquiet with the defined and narrow theology being promulgated by the centre, and a willingness – indeed, an eagerness – to engage with vibrant Baptist traditions from elsewhere in the world that happen not to fit the offered mould exactly, has led many significant individuals and organizations to be more open to a broader tradition of Baptist thought and life than is offered by the centre.

Ignoring the remaining Landmarkist, Primitive and Fundamentalist Baptist groups – which are significant numerically, but offer little of interest to the student of Baptist theology currently – the remainder of North American Baptist life is more generous, more varied and more international in outlook, and also occasionally somewhat distorted by defining itself against the SBC (in much the same way that minority Baptist denominations in southern Europe are occasionally somewhat distorted by defining themselves against Roman Catholicism: a culturally overwhelming alternative tradition is bound to shape a group's self-presentation somewhat). African-American Baptists are producing gifted theologians, although so far, fairly or unfairly, only Martin Luther King has attracted a significant secondary literature; Canadian Baptists seem to struggle to emerge from the overbearing shadow cast over them from the South. Baptist theology in North America seems, to this outsider, pregnant and unstable: some things seemingly cannot stand; others seem more than ready to burst into full bloom. I suspect the coming decades will be exhilarating, painful, creative, destabilizing and, above all, interesting.

Chapter 3

Baptists Beyond North America in the Modern Period

British Baptist Life and thought from 1800

In the first chapter, I left the British Baptist movement at a moment when it was gaining strength from the evangelical revival. The growth was to continue throughout the nineteenth century, peaking in 1906, with a recorded 410,766 members in 2,811 churches in the Baptist Union of Great Britain (which in practice counted most of the English churches, many of the Welsh and virtually none of the Scottish, as members). The membership had at that point doubled in forty years, but then began a long, slow decline through the twentieth century which was, however, less pronounced among Baptists than any other historic denomination in Britain (the first decade of the twenty-first century has seen British Baptist numbers become at least static, and probably even slightly increase). If the figure derived from Rippon's tables of 30,000 members in 1798 is at all correct, it is clear that, as for their American co-religionists, the nineteenth century was a period of massive growth for British Baptists.

Unlike the American story, however, it was also a time of increasing structural unity. The Particular Baptists founded a Union in 1813, which initially achieved little, but was profoundly reorganized in 1832 (with, significantly, the removal of any specifically Calvinistic doctrinal commitments at a time when unity with the New Connexion was being widely discussed) and became a more significant and vibrant body. New Connexion churches did in fact join, forming a separate association within the Union, and the Union had several presidents (serving annual terms) from the General Baptist ranks. In 1891, following a five-year process of resolutions and structural realignments, the two ancient Baptist denominations were fully united. In Scotland, a Baptist Union came into being in 1843, growing out of earlier foundations of a home mission society and an association; however, it collapsed in 1856, but was succeeded by the foundation of the present Baptist Union of Scotland in 1869.

All of this took place against a background, particularly in the first half of the century, of idealistic visions of pan-evangelical unity, stretching from the founding of the London Missionary Society (LMS) in 1795 and the British and Foreign Bible Society in 1804, down to the formation of the Evangelical Alliance (EA) in 1846. The feelings of those involved concerning evangelical unity can be judged from some of the comments made at the time, whether Bogue's famous sermon describing the founding of the LMS as 'The Funeral of Bigotry', or Edward Norris Kirk hailing the EA as 'the death of sectarianism'. Unity was in the cause of spiritual and social transformation, and that transformation was perceived to be possible if unity was achieved – the anti-slavery movement is only the most obvious example. British evangelicals, Baptists included, believed they were better together, and acted on that belief.

Full Baptist involvement in pan-evangelical organizations and campaigns raised issues, of course. If Baptists would never accept the establishment of the Anglican Church as legitimate, they were learning to accept that at least some congregations of the established church were in some sense true Christian churches. Such recognition was, of course, present from the beginnings of British Baptist life in the distinctive stance taken by the Jacob-Lathrop-Jessey church, which was the origin of so many of the founders of the Particular Baptist movement. It was also made easier by the gradual dismantling of some of the more straightforwardly oppressive elements of the Anglican settlement: between 1812 and 1828 the old Clarendon Code was finally repealed, for instance. The question of baptism was a further problem, however, as it was in the US: could Baptists work with those they believed to be unbaptized, on account of their practice of paedobaptism?

In England there was a long history of cooperation, and even of dual-polity churches, stretching back to Jessey (again) and Bunyan. The making of common cause in dissent, and shared evangelical experience, meant that pan-evangelical work was not radically new or unimaginable. A further impetus was given by the theological context of the first half of the nineteenth century: the rise of Tractarianism within the Church of England created a profound aversion among (almost) all evangelicals to any sort of sacramentalism. Baptism was therefore downgraded to an act of witness, at best an enacted sermon. Perhaps the most obvious result of this weakening of baptismal theology among British Baptists was the widespread adoption of the open communion position (i.e., the position that all who profess faith may share around the Lord's Table, regardless of baptismal status), with the decisive arguments coming on the basis of shared evangelical experience in Robert Hall's *On the Terms of Communion* (1815), but the debate continuing until the 1840s, when fear of sacramentalism made Hall's position much more attractive. (The paradoxical result of this, that English Baptists came to have a lower view of the importance of baptism than almost any other tradition, will be discussed in detail in Chapter 5 below).

With the beginnings of the ecumenical movement in the twentieth century, the question of baptism came to prominence again. J. H. Shakespeare, as secretary of the Baptist Union from 1898–1924, was committed to an ecumenical vision; in this, however, he appeared out of step with the majority of the denomination, and his successor, M. E. Aubrey, worked to re-establish confidence in denominational distinctives. British Baptist attitudes to the ecumenical developments of the last century have probably been more positive than those of many of their co-religionists (with the BUGB being generally more positive than the Scottish Union), but have been marked repeatedly by concerns over baptism, over the generally liberal theology of the formal ecumenical instruments and over shared organizational membership with the Roman Catholic Church. (Baptists have also been somewhat impatient of the generally top-down method of ecumenical working, seeing local congregations united in mission as being far more important.)

The towering figure in British Baptist life in the nineteenth century, of course, was Charles Haddon Spurgeon, who was famously involved in controversy over baptismal theology and ecumenical relations. He opposed the doctrine of baptismal regeneration, of course, but attacked the evangelical party of the Church of England far more than the Tractarian party. His point, put rather simply, was that the authorized liturgy for infant baptism in the *Book of Common Prayer* declared baptismal regeneration in forthright terms. Tractarians were at least being faithful to the doctrines encapsulated in the liturgy – 'I hate their doctrine', Spurgeon declared, 'but I love their honesty'. As to the evangelicals, he was blunt: 'I impeach before the bar of universal Christendom, these men, who knowing that baptism does not regenerate, yet declare in public that it does'.[1] Spurgeon pressed the point in later sermons, including a direct appeal to evangelical clergy in the established church to leave. Unsurprisingly, such a direct assault on the integrity of other members led to his being required to resign from the Evangelical Alliance.

It was not just Anglicans that attracted Spurgeon's censure; he instituted the most famous doctrinal controversy in British Baptist life when he turned his fire on his co-religionists in the 'Down Grade' Controversy, named after an article which appeared in *Sword and Trowel* (Spurgeon's house journal) in March 1887. The original article was wide-ranging, attacking prayerless churches, worldly ministers and general doctrinal decay; as the controversy went on, the question of doctrine came to eclipse the others. From 1887 to his death in 1892, Spurgeon published something on the issue almost every month. He demanded that the Baptist Union adopt a formal doctrinal statement; when it hesitated, he withdrew from membership (a statement was in fact proposed to Spurgeon by representatives of the Union in 1888, but by then he was uninterested in healing the breach). Spurgeon, for whatever reason (several have been proposed) kept his accusations at a very general level, refusing to identify ministers he regarded as suspect, and not often specifying even the doctrines about which he was concerned, making it difficult to evaluate the justness of his attack. Where specific cases are known, or can be guessed, however, it seems that while there were some instances of cause for concern, Spurgeon was, just as often, over-hasty.

To take only two examples, Spurgeon was known to find the views of Samuel Cox, pastor of a church in Nottingham, unacceptable. Cox had published *Salvator Mundi* in 1877, arguing for a 'wider hope' – that is, universal salvation. Spurgeon's concern that

Cox remained in the Baptist Union – and, because of the lack of any doctrinal statement, could not be censured by the Union – seems appropriate in the theological climate of the day, where universalism was not unknown, but generally regarded by evangelicals as a dangerous and extreme idea far beyond the bounds of orthodoxy. A second plausible candidate for Spurgeon's ire, however, is W. E. Blomfield, sometime assistant to S. H. Booth, who was secretary of the Baptist Union, and who had apparently supplied Spurgeon with further evidence as to the rightness of his concerns over the general loss of orthodoxy in the denomination before he went public. In 1885, Booth had sought to dismiss his assistant on grounds of unorthodoxy; he failed and was compelled to resign from his pastorate as a result. It seems likely that, in passing evidence for burgeoning unorthodoxy to Spurgeon, he would have mentioned this recent incident. All later judgement, and what evidence we have in print of Blomfield's teachings, suggest that he was doctrinally orthodox by any reasonable standard: he had a habit of illustrating points by citing modern authors of questionable orthodoxy (such as F. D. Maurice and George Eliot), and had adopted an apologetic style of trying to make old doctrines comprehensible; but it is hardly fair criticism of a preacher to note his attempts to make his points intelligible and plausible in the cultural context in which he finds himself. Booth was later reconciled to both Blomfield and the church, suggesting his own awareness that his accusations had been unfair.

Spurgeon, for all his homiletic brilliance and organizational efficiency, was no theologian; his own beliefs were closely akin to Fuller's evangelical Calvinism, but he was publicly proud to be the successor of John Gill's pulpit. He regarded himself as standing in an unbroken line of succession with the Puritans, but he did not understand the twists and turns that had taken place in Reformed theology since then. In particular, he seems simply unaware of the rupture caused by the evangelical doctrine of immediate assurance, which was of immense significance for pastoral practice, and which Spurgeon accepted without demur or any understanding that it was just different from what his favourite writers had taught. He read widely in contemporary theology, but failed to understand the subtleties of what he read (he made no distinction between Arianism and Unitarianism, for instance, regularly using the former term to refer to the Unitarians of his own day). As with Booth's judgement on Blomfield, it seems likely that Spurgeon was as often reading and hearing younger ministers expressing old truths in a new register, and mistaking what he heard for a departure from orthodoxy, as he was finding true evidence for a downgrade in orthodoxy.

That said, there were of course theological developments in British Baptist life over the century. Biblical criticism was recognized and acknowledged, although always with caution; one can find several key leaders, from F. W. Gotch in a presidential address to the Union in 1869 to John Clifford in his widely popular *Inspiration and Authority of the Bible* (1892, 1895: 2nd Edition), essaying the idea that Christ himself is the crucial authority for Christians, mediated through the Scriptures. This was entirely in accord with the Declaration of Principle of the Union, and allowed a certain space to entertain and explore critical ideas without the fundamentals of faith and morals being challenged thereby. In 1918, one of Spurgeon's students, W. Y. Fullerton, would announce in his capacity as president of the Baptist Union that 'our men are true to the evangelical faith in the broad sense, while not out of touch with the thought of the day'[2] This captured the settled mind of the Union better than Spurgeon's lack of understanding of intellectual currents and far better than any fearful defensiveness.

This Christocentric evangelicalism, open to, but critical of, contemporary thought, would represent the mainstream of British Baptist theology through the coming century also, notwithstanding the development of a small fundamentalist tradition in the 1920s, and a broadening to encompass traditions more liberal than Clifford or Fullerton would have found comfortable at times in the second half of the twentieth century. It is perhaps significant, however, that the greatest theological flashpoint of the twentieth century concerned Christology, rather than (say) ecumenism, charismatic renewal, or biblical criticism. With retrospect, Michael Taylor's 1971 Assembly address, under the given title 'How much of a man was Jesus Christ?' appears (at least from the written text) to be an example of someone whose Christian commitment cannot be questioned, wrestling, perhaps unwisely, in public with theological questions that are, at that point, somewhat beyond his grasp. Fairly or not, however, he was heard to be questioning, even denying, the deity of Christ, and it became clear from the reaction, and from the overwhelming support for Cyril Black's motion at the next Assembly (1,800 for; 46 against; 72 abstaining), that this, of all the traditional questions and hesitations of liberal theology, was the one that British Baptists would not begin to entertain.

Ernest Payne, Union secretary, described this as 'a lurch to the right'; Black, as president, saw it differently: it was rather the case that Baptists 'on the ground' were rather more evangelical than the Union's leadership, and that the affair was a healthy, if painful, reminder of that fact (I drew the parallel with slightly later events in the SBC in the previous chapter). The second half of the twentieth century witnessed a general growth in confidence and numbers among the evangelical wing of British Christianity, dating perhaps from Billy Graham's Harringay missions of 1954, carried forward by powerful and gifted leaders such as John Stott or Martyn Lloyd-Jones and further encouraged by the largely successful integration of the new vigour of the charismatic renewal into evangelical church life. Baptists perhaps shared disproportionately in this growth, being the most monolithically evangelical of the mainstream denominations in Britain. At the end of the twentieth century, British Baptist worship was generally charismatic in style, if not always open to the public exercise of spiritual gifts, and British Baptist spirituality and theology had accommodated themselves to this new reality.

Interestingly, the Baptist contribution to the British theological academy in the twentieth century was uneven. Throughout the century, Baptists produced excellent biblical scholars in numbers, from H. H. Rowley and H. Wheeler Robinson in the first half of the century to George Beasley-Murray and Ron Clements, both of whom were still active into the 1990s. The same may be said of church historians, with the great W. T. Whitley active in 1900, and David Bebbington, the most eminent of several current writers. If we look for doctrinal theologians, however, it is difficult to think of a Baptist contributor of any real note before Paul Fiddes, whose publishing career dates from the 1980s. This reflects the general pattern of recognized scholarship among the broader British evangelical community through the century: contributions to biblical scholarship abounded, but from P. T. Forsyth (d. 1921) to Alister McGrath (who published his first book in 1985), there are few, if any, evangelical theologians of real note in Britain.

Why might this be? The climate of academic theology in Britain in the mid-century was inhospitable to anyone from a more conservative background, focusing as it did on doctrinal criticism; that said, evangelical – and Baptist – biblical scholars learnt to accommodate themselves to the practices of higher criticism and to use the methodologies to defend conclusions that, if not identical to the easy assumptions of two centuries before, were at least recognizably committed to a traditional faith. Theologians from these traditions did not discover the same ability to indwell the prevailing intellectual mores. It is of note, in this respect, that Fiddes's DPhil was in a biblical field, although with a string of significant publications in the later 1980s he established himself as one of Britain's leading systematic theologians, not just a major Baptist figure. A near-contemporary of Fiddes, the Congregationalist Colin Gunton blazed a similar trail and taught many who would teach doctrine in Baptist contexts around the turn of the century: Nigel Wright, John Colwell, Graham Watts (all teaching at Spurgeon's College at various points) – and, indeed, the present author.

Perhaps the problem runs deeper than this, however. The intellectual energy of the English Baptists in the nineteenth century was being poured into social and political issues. From emancipation and voting reform in the early part of the century, through prison reform and poor law reform, to temperance movements and the ongoing Baptist support for the Liberal party at elections, national issues of social morality concerned Baptist leaders and churches endlessly. At a congregational level, involvement in local society in various ways was equally common. Spurgeon was far from the only Baptist to found an orphanage; many churches offered free elementary schooling to young people; some leaders, such as J. C. Carlile, became involved in labour and union issues. Perhaps the most interesting example of this local social concern was the work of F. B. Meyer at Melbourne Hall, where a remarkable network of auxiliary church organizations combined with Meyer's adoption of direct gospel appeals after the pattern of his friend Dwight Moody, created an effective evangelistic context for the local church. This pattern, of auxiliary societies as doors into the church fellowship, became a standard model of Baptist local mission into the twentieth century. Thoughtful Baptists were engaged in local church ministry, and so finding practical ways of living out the gospel; the luxury of philosophical reflection was not one they allowed themselves.

The Development of Baptist Life in Continental Europe

Although Baptists trace their beginnings to continental Europe – Smyth and Helwys in Amsterdam – and have at least something in common with some of the older Anabaptist traditions (for more on which see later in this chapter), the beginnings of lasting Baptist work in Europe come rather later in time. Johann Gerhard Oncken (1800–84) is usually credited with founding Baptist work on the continent; this is not quite true – the Scotsman Robert Haldane emigrated to Geneva in 1816 and influenced the founding of French-speaking Baptist congregations both there and in France. Oncken in fact corresponded with Haldane and received support from societies in which he was involved; his mission was independent, though, and its sheer scale dwarfs anything achieved by his Scottish mentor – or indeed by any other European evangelist of the day. He was already a successful missionary when he came to Baptist convictions and, after some delay, was baptized (with six others) in 1824. The seven formed the first German Baptist church, which immediately called Oncken as elder. The church grew to number many hundreds, and Oncken personally, or those he sent out, converted tens of thousands across Europe from Scandinavia to the Balkans. When Oncken died, there were 165 member congregations of the Union he had founded. (I will say a little more about Oncken's career in Chapter 6 below.)

Undoubtedly, Oncken was a brilliant organizer; he was also desirous of maintaining control over his churches. He tried, unsuccessfully by the end, to maintain the position that his own Hamburg church was in fact the only church in the Union, and that all other congregations were mission stations under its jurisdiction; his mission inevitably reached first to the German émigrés in any given country, and so tended to impose Germanic ideals and practices on the churches of the Union – even sometimes seeking to insist that services were conducted in German, not in the local vernacular. Problems like this led to a breakaway Association of Latvian Baptists in the 1880s. Whatever faults or problems may be identified, however, it remains true that the Baptist witness in a dozen or more European countries owes its origins to Oncken's vision, energy and mission.

Theologically, both Haldane and Oncken were committed to an evangelical Calvinism. Both worked comfortably with non-Baptist evangelical bodies – Haldane helping to run pan-evangelical mission societies such as the Continental Society (which for a while employed Oncken), and Oncken drawing support extensively from various groups, some Baptist but some not: his principal supporters over the years would seem to have been the American Baptist Foreign Mission Society and the (pan-evangelical) Bible Society in Edinburgh. Haldane became involved in controversies with the British and Foreign Bible Society (BFBS), from which the Edinburgh organization seceded: on the one hand, he advocated a developed doctrine of plenary verbal inspiration – then a novelty within the evangelical tradition, at least in the sense that the question had never been so starkly posed, and so decisively answered, before; on the other, he was profoundly concerned with the BFBS's willingness to include the apocryphal writings with Bibles it published for circulation on the continent. Both Oncken and Haldane were involved in the founding of the Evangelical Alliance in 1846, however.

European Baptist life thus had its origins in a Calvinistic and pan-evangelical tradition. Its growth has largely been marked by continuous contexts of persecution, formal or informal. While in Britain the ability of the state church to persecute was all but eroded by the 1830s (in England; the Presbyterian Church of Scotland generally showed itself less willing to oppress other [Protestant] Christians than the Church of England), problems remained in most countries on the continental mainland. Historically, Roman Catholic and Orthodox nations tended to see their national identity as tied up with the national religion, and so tended to legislate against Protestant and evangelical movements, including Baptists. Even when formal church-state ties were ended, as in France in 1905, suspicion and informal local opposition and persecution often remained. Historically Protestant nations sometimes offered little better: in Germany, for example, Oncken was imprisoned more than once for his faith and preaching, and the notion that Lutheran and Roman Churches remain established, supported by taxation and privileged in law remains strong. To take only one example, in recent memory, a scholar's appointment to a university chair was delayed by years because of his Baptist convictions.[3] While such cases do not represent the norm, they do indicate the level of ignorance and residual persecution that Baptists can face, not just in Germany, but across the European continent.

Unsurprisingly, the totalitarian regimes of recent European history were often at least as inhospitable to Baptists. The German Baptists actually fared rather well compared to many others, and even after the end of World War II, a surprising degree of loyalty remained. Visiting German Baptist pastors in 1948, Leonard Champion records in his diary that while they were prepared to admit that a telegram congratulating Hitler on his escape from assassination in 1944 was a mistake, they were still reluctant to condemn him outright. Perhaps this is unsurprising: Hitler had allowed them to worship according to their conscience. Baptists suffering under Soviet oppression could not say the same.

The separatism of the American Landmarkist tradition is not unknown within European life, but the shared context of persecution with other minority evangelical groups has meant that the British tradition of making common cause with fellow sufferers, and emphasizing that which unites the free churches rather than that which divides, has been a more common theological response. Particularly interesting in this respect, perhaps, is the relationship of Baptists with those Anabaptist groups who survived (often relentless) persecution. John Smyth, of course, having founded the Baptist movement, repented of that act and joined the local Mennonite congregation; and there is credible, if not incontrovertible, evidence of some measure of continuing interaction between English Baptists and Dutch Mennonites through the seventeenth century. Rippon listed Mennonite churches in his *Annual Register*, implying that he regarded them as genuine Baptist churches who should be welcomed within the associational structures that he was trying to promote; similarly, when Fuller was seeking support for the nascent Baptist Missionary Society, an approach was made to the Mennonites for funds.

When Baptists begin an aggressive programme of church planting in continental Europe, however, the context changed: Baptists and Mennonites could now potentially find themselves competing for the same seekers, and so operating in conditions where disputes and pamphlet wars similar to those which divided Baptists and Quakers in seventeenth-century England could arise. In the absence of a Cromwellian commonwealth offering de facto general toleration to Protestants, however, such adversarial relationships did not arise: in the USSR, for instance, the two denominations were forced into the same structure, the All-Union Council of Evangelical Christians-Baptists (established 1944, and shared with Pentecostal denominations); while organizational unity was here a government imposition rather than an ecclesial decision, the fact that it was able to work in some measure points to the ability of the denominations to find a common mind and vision out of their common heritage.

In theological terms, have Baptists in Europe developed a distinctive vision of what it is to be Baptist? The story of the Baptist Theological Seminary, founded in 1949 in Rüschlikon, Switzerland, and translated and relocated to Prague in 1996–7 (where it was renamed the International Baptist Theological Seminary, or IBTS), is perhaps instructive. The Rüschlikon seminary was initially funded by the Foreign Mission Board of the American Southern Baptist Convention; this worked successfully for three decades or more, but in the 1980s a series of problems arose. Some were merely financial: changes in the world currency markets rapidly made operating in Switzerland significantly more expensive (in dollar terms) than it had been previously, and this had to be faced. At the same time, changes in the theological position of the SBC, outlined in the previous chapter, led to an increasing tension between the seminary and its major funders. In 1988, control and ownership of the seminary was handed over from the Foreign Mission Board of the SBC to the European Baptist Federation; a fifteen-year transitional funding package was agreed at the same time. However, once under the control of the EBF, the seminary began to be shaped into European patterns of Baptist theology, which were found so alien by the SBC that the transitional funding was withdrawn without warning and at short notice (it is fair to say that the political fallout from this decision, routinely described by Europeans as a reneging on a signed agreement, continues to sour relationships within the Baptist world). Faced with multiple problems stemming from its Swiss location – such as expense, but also access, as the Swiss government was less willing to grant visas, and issues of accreditation of academic awards within the Swiss university system – and a new context of the openness of post-communist central and eastern Europe, the seminary relocated to Prague, and relaunched as the International Baptist Theological Seminary, where it has succeeded in developing a distinctive identity within the Baptist world.

With regard to theological history, two aspects of this story are important. On the one hand, around 1990 there is a fundamental breach between the seminary, which, given its continuing importance, must be regarded as representing the mainstream of European Baptist life, and the SBC. Almost as soon as the seminary began to be shaped by its new EBF owners, the promised funding from the SBC was withdrawn, apparently because the FMB was not prepared to be associated with the teaching now offered in the institution. Of course, any funding agency has both a right and a duty to ensure that its money is being put to the use that it is intended for, and if the FMB found the curriculum being developed at the seminary simply unacceptable, its decision to withdraw funding is entirely defensible. The decision suggests, however, that the teaching introduced under EBF management of the seminary was somehow profoundly alien and offensive to Southern Baptist understandings of the gospel and of ministerial formation. On the other hand, with the relaunch of the seminary as IBTS in Prague, it is no surprise that there was a general and urgent sense of a need for a new theological vision, one that was sufficiently positive and generative to secure an attractive (to students) future identity for the institution, but also one that was sufficiently far from those things urged by the SBC that there could be no suggestion that the withdrawal of funding might actually have succeeded in affecting in any way the curriculum taught in the seminary.

When we also note that at the time all this was happening there was a high-profile and somewhat controversial realignment of Southern Baptist denominational identity, the implications of this story for European Baptist theology are not difficult to predict: there was a widespread and visceral rejection of the visions of what it is to be Baptist that were being promoted within the hierarchy of the Southern Baptist Convention, coupled with a pressing desire to find an alternative vision. It may be, of course, that European Baptist life would have developed in the direction it did regardless of the actions of the SBC; indeed, this is probably true – we should not overestimate the theological effect of a financial decision. Perhaps it is the mode of presentation of the distinctive vision of European Baptist theology that has been most affected: instead of an irenic attempt to minimize distinctives, there has sometimes been a sense of a positive celebration that what is being offered is a different vision of being Baptist from that promoted by the SBC.

All that said, what is this distinctive European vision? I have discussed it at some length in the introduction of this book, and will explore it further in the next chapter, but, briefly, it sees the doctrine that God's primary concern is local churches composed of visible believers as utterly central. This has been developed into an account of Baptist theology which places enormous stress on the church practices: true theology happens within the church; for instance, academic theologians, if they have any role at all, exist in part to resource the decisions of churches and associational bodies, and in part to hear and analyze ecclesial deliberations, which themselves are the basic matter of theology. Baptists, on this view, should almost rejoice in their lack of academically recognized scholars: the academy looks for the wrong things, and so is at best uninteresting and at worst misleading. It is in the local congregation that proper theology – adequate discourse about God – happens.

This is a bold and creative vision, with evident roots in Baptist history. As a Baptist, presently employed by a secular university to teach and research in theological disciplines, I find it difficult to evaluate simply because I am conscious that, if correct, it would raise pressing questions concerning my own current ways of living out my vocation, and I am therefore aware of a strong personal desire that this proposal should be wrong. With such caveats in place, my criticisms of the view would centre on the hard line drawn between academy and church: there are many Baptist theologians, stretching back into the seventeenth century, who have straddled that line in various ways, and so proposing a hard distinction based upon it seems methodologically difficult. That said, the warning that what is good Baptist theology – that is, timely, biblical and useful for the local church – may not be recognized as good theology within the academy is profoundly important for all Baptist scholars.

Baptist Theology in the Majority World

Thus far, my history has been almost confined to the West – in considering Europe, bits of previously communist Europe and Asia have been mentioned, and the existence of the missions movement has been noted. In purely numerical terms, at present, however, the world beyond the West – Latin and South America; Africa; Asia beyond Russia; Australasia beyond Australia and New Zealand – is, if not quite the majority of Baptist witness (the sheer size of the SBC tilts that in favour of the US), certainly the location of greatest growth and diversity.

The history of Baptists in the Majority World generally begins with foreign, usually Western, missions, leading to an indigenous church that gradually begins to find and assert its own identity. Other than the areas of Europe that Oncken evangelized, this has not been the pattern of the stories I have told so far: in Britain and America – and in Germany, through Oncken – Baptists emerged from within the culture, and so Baptist churches were from the first successfully inculturated. In other European countries, Oncken initially sought to impose a culturally German church, leading to unhappiness and even splits such as the breakaway Latvian group mentioned above. That said, Latvia was not so culturally different from Germany that the process of making the churches Latvian was a complex or difficult one; the planting of a British church in India, or an American church in Zimbabwe, was a different story, however.

Two particular issues made the process of inculturation of new churches difficult: the colonial heritage and the flow of finance. Colonialism was not quite universal, of course, but where colonial annexation had happened it brought with it a set of unjust power relations, which enabled easy missionary access but implicated the Christian gospel and its messengers in exploitation and injustice on a massive scale. Generally, mission outreach has happened from rich Western countries to poor southern nations, and so church infrastructures have depended, at least initially, on foreign funding. This inevitably creates tensions – the story of the European Baptist Theological Seminary told above could be repeated many times over, with almost any Western mission organization at times playing the role of the funder that seeks to influence extensively the development of the local church in ways that are perceived to be unhelpful locally. The development of an authentically local theological vision, therefore, has often been hampered by complications arising from post-colonial suspicions, and by the need to break free of any material and personnel support that comes with (formal or informal) strings attached.

Despite such problems, there is no doubt that Baptists in the Majority World are increasingly finding ways of successfully contextualizing and inculturating the Baptist vision; at present, it is probably fair to say that this is happening primarily at the level of practice and secondarily in the context of seminary training. Stories can easily be discovered of distinctively Baptist appropriations of concerns for justice learnt from liberation theology, or of the development of a sexual ethic that sees that horror at polygamy coupled with easy acceptance of divorce is a Western inculturation, and not adequately biblical (the – Baptist – Women's Missionary Union in Zimbabwe, for instance, proposes a set of practices in its published Manual that seem to suggest that polygamy and divorce are alike treated as imperfect accommodations to the hardness of human hearts), or of practices of communal discernment that instantiate Baptist convictions about the mind of Christ being known together in ways explicable to the local culture, or of funerary rites that take seriously traditional beliefs and practices and seek to re-frame them in adequately Christian ways. Such narratives are captured, discussed and re-framed in seminaries, leading to an ongoing dissemination and development of distinctive and local ways of being Baptist.

That said, it is presently difficult to find writers who are interrogating these practices and discussions and forming out of them an account of Baptist theology from an African, Latin American or South East Asian perspective. It may be that it is inappropriate to look for such work: perhaps one of the things being evaluated and found unhelpful is a Western way of practising theology (which, after all, is profoundly shaped by a developed university system that, from Bernard of Clairvaux's criticisms of Peter Lombard down, has had a somewhat uneasy relationship with the church, and particularly with the free churches). Equally, however, it is possible that we simply await the great expositors of non-Western Baptist theology or that the (Western-controlled) academy is somehow preventing their voices from being heard. The place where non-Western Baptists have offered generative and distinctive academic work is, perhaps unsurprisingly, the area of mission; in the next chapter I will discuss briefly African and Latin American missiologists such as Bosch, Costas and Escobar: Baptist writers who offer a new perspective on the academic conversation that grows (in part, at least) from their successful reinterpretation of traditional themes in the light of the communities that formed them.

Chapter 4

Baptist Perspectives on Ecumenical Theology

Introduction

As noted earlier, on most shared ecumenical doctrines, Baptist theology is not distinctive, although the theology of individual Baptists might be. This point has been repeatedly emphasized by Baptist groups in the face of active or threatened persecution, hoping that stressing their basic Christian orthodoxy will save them from the ire of their oppressors. The most significant example might be the Second London Confession of 1677, which is a Baptist rewriting of the famous Presbyterian Westminster Confession of 1646 (in fact the Baptist version draws on the Congregationalist revisiting of Westminster, the Savoy Declaration of 1658). While there is no slavish following of Westminster, the Confession was clearly designed to emphasize Baptist unity with other nonconformists of the day: while they were not afraid to believe that they could express certain matters concerning salvation better than the Westminster Divines had managed, essentially they stressed their unity and conformity with the broad Protestant tradition on most matters of doctrine.

In the English tradition, this broad Protestant unity was recognized in the Act of Toleration of 1689. Presbyterians and Congregationalists would be exempted from the provisions of the Clarendon Code (and other similar legislation) if they would take certain oaths of loyalty, and certify their acceptance of thirty-six of the Thirty-Nine Articles of Religion of the Church of England (they were allowed to demur from Articles 34–36, which deal with ecclesiology); Baptists were allowed to accept only thirty-five, being allowed to dissent also from Article 27, which affirmed the propriety of infant baptism. These two examples show that, even at the time of the most heightened awareness of religious differences in England, there was an acceptance that most doctrines were shared, with only some dispute about the proper governance of the church, and the proper subjects of baptism, separating the denominations. (The Articles in fact affirm Calvinist doctrines, but the Church of England had long since ceased to be committed to predestination, and there seemed to be a general assumption that a General Baptist, or indeed a Quaker, could sign the Articles in good conscience.)

In the account of Baptist theology I give in this book, many things are simply assumed as being uncontentious. Baptists accept, without hesitation, received ecumenical positions on many issues, or share equally in ecumenical debates. There is not, for instance, a distinctive Baptist doctrine of the person of Christ, and Baptists would have the same variety of positions as other broadly evangelical Protestants on the question of how best to describe the work of Christ. To be specific, there is little or no discussion in the remainder of this book of: the Trinity, the perfections of God, the doctrine of the divine decrees, creation, the doctrine of humanity, sin and the Fall, the person and work of Christ or eschatology. It is not that Baptists have failed to address these concepts; but their – our; I have written on more than one of the topics – contributions have not, as far as I can see, given any indication that there might be a distinctively Baptist position. That said, brief surveys are perhaps in order here to demonstrate the point. That is the work of this chapter.

Of necessity, the discussion in this chapter moves quickly, and assumes a certain familiarity with the broad contours of Christian doctrine, and its recent history. The reader who is prepared to accept the claim that, on matters other than ecclesiology, Baptists are not generally distinct from other Protestants might therefore wish to pass over this material to get to the more positive accounts of Baptist distinctives in the chapters that follow.

The Doctrine of God

Baptist writers in the seventeenth century generally affirmed the classical doctrine of the Trinity without exploring it at any length. The biblicist anti-Trinitarianism of the times did not pass them by, however: Matthew Caffyn, a significant leader among the General Baptists, was accused in the 1690s of denying the deity of Christ; although the facts of the case are less clear than many historians have represented, he at least denied the worth (indeed, the logical coherence) of the Athanasian Creed, thus displaying an unhappiness with a classic statement of traditional doctrine, albeit one that has come in for steady criticism in recent centuries.[1] Come 1719 and the Salters' Hall Synod, almost all General Baptist ministers present refused to subscribe to any confession of faith that was not merely biblical in language, and over the eighteenth century, many of the churches of the General Baptist denomination drifted into Unitarianism. The Particular Baptists remained more generally orthodox, as did the New Connexion, and most of the Baptist movements in the American colonies.

This general orthodoxy remained the norm until the twentieth century, although it is notable that Baptists did not generally insist on conformity to the ecumenical creeds, and so formal tests of Trinitarian orthodoxy may not have been required often. In the twentieth century, Baptist theologians can be found following the broad lines of ecumenical debates: in the context of the doctrinal criticism which (in this area) reached its most notorious height in 1977, with the publication of *The Myth of God Incarnate*, Baptists could be found struggling in public with the problem of making sense of classical language in contemporary thought and offending more traditional believers as they did so (Michael Taylor's 1971 Baptist Union of Great Britain (BUGB) presidential address is the obvious example). By the time of the 'Trinitarian revival' of the last decades of the century, Baptists could be found on every side of the discussions: eagerly endorsing, and indeed making perceptive and positive contributions to, relational Trinitarianism (see, e.g. Paul Fiddes's *Participating in God*[2]); generally welcoming the movement while raising questions (see, e.g. Stanley Grenz, *Rediscovering the Triune God*); or expressing strong reservations with the new perspectives (see, e.g. Holmes, *The Holy Trinity*). One might suspect that a commitment to congregationalism, and thus to the primary theological importance of relationships within the local church, would make Baptists more open to some strands of the Trinitarian revival, but there does not seem to be very much data to support such a suspicion: Baptist theologians who have written on the Trinity have not visibly been more positive than others; and the occasional publications that narrate the attempt to consciously apply contemporary Trinitarian theology to local church life do not generally appear to have considered Baptist churches.

Baptist contributions to other, less widespread contemporary debates about the Trinity display the same pattern. The (to outsiders, idiosyncratic at best) American evangelical attempt to use questions of Trinitarian relatedness to attack or support positions concerning gender relationships has attracted contributors from the Baptist world, particularly from the SBC, but they neither consistently support one side of the debate nor bring a specifically Baptist contribution to it.[3] Beyond occasional parenthetic comments concerning church government, Baptist contributions here could equally well have been made by a member of the Presbyterian Church of America. Baptists have not been neglectful of Trinitarian theology, and some have made significant contributions, but their contributions have not always supported the same positions, and have not generally been distinctively Baptist in shape.

Much the same might be said of other aspects of the doctrine of God. Baptists generally assumed the traditional doctrine of God when it was generally assumed; although often lacking in formal theological training, there is considerable evidence that Baptist autodidacts regularly achieved an astonishingly competent grasp of the contours and details of classical theology (Thomas Monck's astonishing *Cure for the Cankering Error of the New Eutychians* [1673] is eloquent testimony to this point, containing an exposition of classical theology proper, Trinitarian doctrine and Christology, that, if lacking any originality, offers an remarkably thorough and competent account of the key points of technical theology).

John Gill's *Body of Doctrinal Divinity* (1769) discussed no less than twenty-seven different attributes of God, which is unusually expansive, but what he taught was recognizably within the Reformed tradition of his day. His location of the doctrine of the divine decrees under the head of 'the internal works of God' was more unusual, although not unique, in the day; it could be read in two different ways. On the one hand, Gill is remembered as a proponent of hyper-Calvinism, and it could be argued that tying the doctrine of the decrees more closely to the doctrine of God represents a strand of that tradition that seeks to heighten the eternal distinction between the elect and the reprobate, insisting on a lasting difference that precedes their coming to faith. Alternatively, and perhaps more charitably, Gill might be read as facing up to the question posed most acutely by Barth, concerning the relation of the divine decrees to the perfections of God's life. In either case, there is little or nothing in Gill's doctrine that is explicitly or distinctively Baptist; he is a brilliant, if conservative, expositor of a broader Reformed tradition.

After Kant and Schleiermacher, traditional accounts of the perfections became harder to hold to; Baptists were perhaps a generally conservative community, and these challenges took some decades to find their way into Baptist theology, but find their way they did. The nineteenth-century debate over the personality of God formed part of the apologetic of E. G. Robinson (1815–94), who taught variously at Rochester, Brown and Chicago, and inspired a generation of Northern Baptist theologians to engage seriously, if critically with contemporary German theology. Among his students, G. W. Northrup of Chicago made much of the ethical perfection of God (as a German mediating tradition that found its best exponent in Isaak Dorner had, and as P. T. Forsyth did in England): a personalist doctrine of God at least invites the doctrine of divine perfection to be recast into ethical terms, and thus traditional metaphysical perfections such as immutability to be somewhat downplayed.

Northrup predated slightly Augustus H. Strong, long-time president of Rochester, and the most intellectually able Baptist exponent of personalism. Strong's 1907 *Systematic Theology* is a genuinely great book, standing alongside Gill's *Doctrinal Divinity* and few others as a truly significant systematic survey by a Baptist. Strong unquestionably made a real contribution to the development of American theology with his thorough development of a personalist account of God and how that worked through every locus of theology. In all of this, however, Baptists, even Strong, were following, or at best developing, paths worn by German Lutheran and Reformed theologians, paths which, alongside Strong, found their most able expositor in the English-speaking world in P. T. Forsyth. These Baptist writers were part of a broader theological movement, and it is difficult to pinpoint anything specifically Baptist in their appropriation of it.

In the present, Baptists can once again be found on every side of debates in this area. Paul Fiddes might be the most able and convincing proponent of divine passibility in the world today (see particularly his *Creative Suffering of God*), but other Baptists have stoutly defended the opposite point; John Colwell's explorations of divine eternity (see *Actuality and Provisionality*) remain significant, but are not constructed, nor easily presented, as distinctively Baptist. The recently controversial position of open theism has its Baptist proponents – notably Gregory Boyd – but more Baptist critics, some trenchant (e.g. John Piper), some still critical but more nuanced (Roger Olson). Is there a distinctively Baptist contribution to the doctrine of God? There may be, but the evidence seems to suggest that few, if any, Baptist theologians have discovered it.

The Person and Work of Christ

A similar story may be told concerning Christology. Again, Baptists were not immune from the maelstrom of ideas that swirled around the radical hinterland of mid-seventeenth-century English church life. Matthew Caffyn, again, was charged by fellow Baptists with denying the true humanity of Christ, and with Eutyhcianism; there is reason to suppose the charges thus phrased to be false (he argued vociferously for the true human flesh of the Redeemer in protracted and ill-tempered debates with Quakers, including George Fox himself). He certainly held to a rather odd belief concerning the humanity of Christ, however, one probably derived from Menno Simons. Both Menno and Caffyn argued that Christ's human nature was not derived in any part from his mother, but was created *ex nihilo* in heaven, united to the divine Logos and then entered the world by passing through the body of the Blessed Virgin. It seems that Caffyn preached up such ideas, and other Baptists, both General and Particular, took time to warn their congregations against this error.

Apart from such idiosyncrasies, the history of Baptist theology before the nineteenth century is again one of general orthodoxy on matters of Christology, the English General Baptist drift into Unitarianism notwithstanding. Once again, the challenge to the comprehensibility of classical Christian doctrine posed most sharply by Kant, and the brilliant but radical defences offered by Schleiermacher, eventually affected Baptists, although again it took some decades for the effects to be felt, if they were. It is difficult, for example, to find a serious Baptist exponent of kenotic Christology (Alvah Hovey knew and referenced the German tradition of Thomasius and Gess, and indeed the criticisms offered by Dorner, but regarded kenoticism as an unhelpful dead end).

That said, the nineteenth century offered a profound focus on the true humanity of Christ, with a new interest in his inner psychology: to be truly human, he had to feel as we feel, not just share in our ontology. The 'quest for the historical Jesus' that such interest gave rise to did not attract distinguished Baptist contributors, but a similar concern can be seen in the sermons Baptists from across the theological spectrum preached. Christ knew our weaknesses and struggles, and so could both sympathize with us, and could be offered as an example of one who had triumphed in the face of the general vicissitudes of human life: this was a endless theme of Baptist preaching in the later nineteenth century, uniting Spurgeon and Clifford, and Landmarkists with meditating liberals.

One of the more interesting examples of this is the great New York Baptist preacher, Harry Emerson Fosdick, whose Christology has been the subject of some controversy. Fosdick endlessly stressed the true humanity of Christ, drawing constantly on it as a theme for encouragement and inspiration for his hearers: Christ knows our weaknesses and experiences (see, for instance, *The Manhood of the Master*). Fosdick has, however, been regularly accused of an inadequate account of the deity of Christ. The reality is probably not that he intended to change inherited doctrine but that, sharing the anti-metaphysical bent of the age, he struggled to find language to express Christ's deity adequately; in this, of course, he was hardly alone. As already noted, Michael Taylor's address to the BUGB in 1971 can be understood in similar terms.

Of course, other Baptists reacted strongly to any such expressed confusion or difficulty: Spurgeon declared a 'Down Grade'; Fosdick was castigated by the fundamentalists (although, to be fair, he fired the opening shots in that particular battle); and Taylor's speculations had far-reaching consequences in Britain. Once again, however, it is difficult to point to any specifically Baptist component to this debate. Probably the relative balance of 'conservatives' to 'liberals' is somewhat different in the Baptist tradition than in others, with the centre of balance, so to speak, being a more generally conservative position; the arguments deployed on either side, however, are not noticeably different from those employed in other Christian traditions.

Turning to the work of Christ, the Baptist tradition is unusual, although not unique (Anglicanism has evolved to accept a similar breadth) in having both Calvinist and Arminian strands, not just in its origin, but in contemporary theological expression (Roger Olson would be an example of a contemporary Baptist theologian who places much stress on his adherence to classical Arminianism) – although questions concerning the doctrines of grace have generally, rightly or wrongly, receded into the background for Baptists, as for most others. Baptists have been more energetically engaged on questions of soteriology over the years than on most other theological topics, perhaps an indication of the missionary impetus at the heart of the tradition; that said, their debates have once again merely paralleled wider ecumenical debates.

This is true of the Calvinist-Arminian debates of the seventeenth century, and of arguments over the 'modern question' and duty-faith in the eighteenth and nineteenth centuries. Andrew Fuller learnt his evangelical Calvinism from the Congregationalist Jonathan Edwards; and the missionary theology, as much as the missionary practice, of the nineteenth-century American Baptists was largely borrowed from Finney. Hyper-Calvinism, understood as opposition to duty-faith, lasted longer among the Baptists than other denominations (most notably, of course, in the continuing existence of Primitive Baptist churches today), but the arguments deployed in its defence have not been noticeably different.

Fuller was involved in another, rather different, controversy over the work of Christ, against Baptists who had adopted Sandemanian tenets, particularly Archibald McLean. Robert Sandeman, although not from a Baptist background, had advocated a return to various practices which he held to be demonstrably those of the New Testament churches, including, *inter alia*, weekly

Eucharistic celebration, foot-washing and 'the holy kiss'. The form of this appeal, to primitive practice, was powerful for Baptists, and Sandeman gained a number of Baptist followers; the strength was in Scotland, but there were some in London, and in the New World (Isaac Backus wrote against Sandemanian principles in 1767), and even the famous Welsh preacher Christmas Evans was swayed to Sandemanian principles for a period. Sandemanians held tenaciously to one idiosyncratic soteriological point, that faith is mere intellectual assent. Belief that the gospel history is in fact true is all that is required for salvation (and thus, for Sandemanian Baptists, the only condition for baptism). Against this, Backus and Fuller would emphasize the place of the will in true saving faith, which is a conviction of the cosmic importance and personal effectiveness of the gospel, not just of its historic truth.

The Sandemanian tradition remained influential in Scots Baptist life into the middle of the nineteenth century; the (paedobaptist, independent) chapels founded by Sandeman lasted longer, however, the tradition only finally disappearing in the last years of the twentieth century. While Baptists found Sandemanian primitivism congenial, and while Fuller's rebuttal of the tradition remains the classic criticism, once again the debate is not a distinctively Baptist one.

Nineteenth-century unhappiness with traditional penal substitutionary accounts of the Atonement finds its way into Baptist debate: Fuller, already, was offering creative recastings of soteriology which avoided, or at least de-emphasized, the penal element. In America, the development of Alvah Hovey of Newton is particularly interesting: in the first edition of his *Manual of Systematic Theology*, published in 1877, he used propitiation as the organizing principle of Atonement doctrine; twenty-three years later, in the second edition, propitiation was not absent, but was relegated to being a qualifying or illustrative account of the central understanding of atonement as Christ's self-sacrifice. The emphasis was no longer on the turning aside of the wrath of an angry deity; rather the noble act of a loving Saviour was to the fore.

In the same year as Hovey's first edition, the English Baptist pastor Samuel Cox had caused a significant stir by proposing universal salvation. His book *Salvator Mundi* did not so much offer a defence of universalism as speculate about the possibility, but this was more than enough to cause scandal. A belief in universal divine benevolence, coupled with an anti-supernaturalism, which found notions such as the transfer of guilt difficult to comprehend, had led to a sea-change in theological attempts to narrate the saving work of Christ. Of course, once again there were conservative voices – Spurgeon, not alone in England, but the most vociferous and tenacious; many associated with the old Landmark traditions in the US. Equally, a few Baptists attempted to discover positions that seemed more theologically adequate than the new focus on Christ's self-sacrificial act and culturally more relevant than the old account of an angry deity demanding blood. A. H. Strong is again, perhaps, the most interesting in purely intellectual terms. His earlier published accounts of soteriology offer a position that might be described as a species of Grotianism, in which God can and does forgive sinners out of mere benevolence, but must also make a public demonstration of the true seriousness of sin in order to uphold the moral order of the universe, and this is made on the cross. He moves later, however, to a distinctive position of his own in which atonement is a universal and eternal reality, arranged and completed by the ethical union of the eternal Logos with the totality of sinful humanity. Such a view accords well with Strong's personalism, but also addresses creatively the standard nineteenth-century concern as to how a contingent fact of history (the Crucifixion) can be of eternal and decisive significance.

In such changing visions of the Atonement, there is also, of course, a dispute happening about the nature of sin: is sin a crime of infinite seriousness against a holy God, or is it something softer than this, a failure of human beings to live up to their true nature, perhaps? Strong's most influential student, Walter Rauschenbusch, took this debate in another direction again, with his account of the 'social gospel', so influential on Martin Luther King, Jr, among others. Rauschenbusch is another of the relatively few Baptists who can claim to have been influential on the theological academy beyond their denomination.

Rauschenbusch ministered in the Hell's Kitchen area of New York (and later joined the faculty of Rochester); there he confronted first-hand systemic social ills and began to perceive that 'sin' was something wider than the individual failures of individual people. God is personal, better understood as 'Father' than 'Ruler'; sin is personal selfishness, but is also instantiated in 'super-personal' forces in society, which, for salvation to be complete, must be brought under the rule of Christ. Even the Crucifixion was the result not just of individual failings, but of such societal forces as 'religious bigotry', 'mob spirit,' and 'militarism'. The Kingdom of God is a social reality that will only be fully realized in the Eschaton, but can be anticipated and partially realized by social action today. Rauschenbusch became the acknowledged leader of the social gospel movement (and King its most distinguished student), but the movement itself was neither natively (Rauschenbusch was preceded by Congregationalists such as Washington Gladden) nor exclusively Baptist.

In the twentieth century, debates over how the Atonement is best understood continued. Baptists made distinguished contributions (most notably, perhaps, Fiddes's *Past Event and Present Salvation*) on various sides. The question of the extent of salvation in a multi-faith world has become particularly live since 1970, and again Baptists have engaged on either side of the issue. Baptists have always been profoundly interested in soteriology, but there is, once again, no distinctively Baptist soteriology that commands general assent.

Creation and Eschatology

Eschatology was a profoundly contested issue among the seventeenth-century English Protestant radicals who gave birth to the Baptist movement; Diggers, Levellers, Ranters, Fifth Monarchists and Muggletonians were all committed to particular views on the subject. For most of them, of course, the heart of their views were the immanent coming of the Kingdom as a political reality in Britain and what needed to be done to hasten or prepare for that. Many of the early English Baptists were significantly involved with some of these groups, notably the Levellers and Fifth Monarchists; that said, like many others who were initially caught up in apocalyptic fervour at the time of the regicide, most Baptists gradually came to distance themselves from such politicized eschatologies.

The broader eschatology of the Puritan movement, largely inherited by Baptists on the one hand, and the eighteenth-century evangelicals on the other, was literalist and traditional. After death, the soul entered into a conscious anticipation of its eternal destiny, either suffering or glory. Earth's history would culminate in the return of Jesus, which was almost universally held to be post-millennial; that is, to follow a thousand-year period of presently unimaginable prosperity and holiness on earth (this derived from Rev. 20.1-6). When Jesus returned, the dead would be raised bodily, the final judgement take place and the Eschaton begin. There was a heightened, but not immanent, expectation of the beginning of these events: typically, Puritans and evangelicals (and with them Baptists) expected the millennium to begin soon, but not within their own lifetimes, with various dates proposed based on analysis of biblical prophecy. Worldwide mission, when it came on the agenda, was often held up as a first moment of progress towards the Eschaton.

In the nineteenth century, initially under the influence of John Nelson Darby, the founder of the Brethren, an alternative, if equally literalist, eschatology began to be popular among conservative Protestants, including Baptists. In this, 'pre-millennial' scheme, Rev. 20.1-6 was interpreted to teach that the thousand-year reign of the saints on earth would follow, not precede, the return of Christ. This view was enshrined in the famous and influential Scofield Reference Bible, which was published in 1909, and sold over two million copies in the next few decades; its importance is not in the details of the predicted eschatological events, but in the cultural mood promoted: post-millennial eschatology sees the culmination of human history as a triumph of civilization, and of Christian mission, and so is fundamentally optimistic about culture; pre-millennial eschatology is fundamentally pessimistic, assuming Christ's return will be a decisive intervention in an increasingly evil and vicious culture. (It is no surprise that the success of Scofield's Bible coincided with World War I, which gave rise to an extremely widespread cultural pessimism, as any student of art or literature can testify.) Pre-milliennialism became common, perhaps normal, among Baptists – particularly among more theologically conservative Baptists – in the US during the twentieth century; it was much less common in the wider world.

Major Baptist denominations have tended, if they have chosen to comment officially on eschatology, to commit themselves to a traditional eschatology without attempting to rule on this debate (e.g. the various editions of the SBC's *Baptist Faith and Message*). Individual Baptist theologians have embraced various positions: A. J. Gordon (1836–95), for example, a significant and energetic pastor in Boston, MA, was an early and extremely vocal supporter of the pre-millennial cause, publishing extensively in support of it (see particularly his *Ecce Venit*); F. B. Meyer was similarly active in promoting pre-millennialism in Britain, where it remained more eccentric. In the twentieth century, some Baptist New Testament scholars, supremely George R. Beasley-Murray (but also Southern Baptists such as Ray Summers), made genuine contributions to the renewal of scholarly interest in New Testament eschatology that followed Schweitzer's devastating critique of *The Quest of the Historical Jesus*. A renewed interest in the genre of apocalyptic literature led these writers to criticize any literalist interpretation of the millennium of Rev. 20 and to stress the in-breaking of the eschatological future into the present order in the resurrection of Jesus, an event which should decisively shape our understanding of our own times.

Baptist theologians have been perhaps less ready to embrace the thoroughgoing turn to eschatology in systematics that followed the publication of Jürgen Moltmann's *Theology of Hope* in 1964. Even Stanley Grenz, who studied under Pannenberg and might thus have been expected to embrace the turn to the future of contemporary German dogmatics, chose not to develop his own thought in such directions. There is, perhaps, a distinctively Baptist form of this turn, however, in some of the Anabaptist-influenced ecclesiologies of recent years: the church is the foretaste of the coming Kingdom, and so lives by different rules, not primarily as an act of withdrawal from culture, but as a prophetic act of witnessing to culture the coming reality.

The history of the doctrine of creation in recent years in perhaps less interesting, but one point is worth making in the context of present hard line stances among certain Baptist groups on an acceptance of the current scientific consensus concerning evolution. The great nineteenth-century controversy over science and religion concerned geology, not biology: Lyell's uniformitarian geology, advanced in three volumes published in 1830–33, popularized the idea that geological features were the products of long ages of natural processes that are still observable today: volcanoes, water erosion, earthquakes and so on. The antiquity of the earth, and the denial of special processes of creation, are thus alike called into question. There were, of course, attempts to harmonize Lyell's theories with biblical authority and theological themes – the most considerable perhaps offered by the English Congregationalist John Pye-Smith who, although most famous for his commitment to the anti-slavery cause, was elected to fellowships in both the Royal Society and the Geological Society in recognition of the quality of his scientific argument on this issue.

In this context, while there was debate about Darwin's ideas (Darwin in fact was influenced by Lyell, and was reading his *Principles of Geology* while on the Beagle), they were neither the first nor the most significant scientific proposals to challenge received theological ideas. By the turn of the century, indeed, novels satirizing the evangelical failure to keep up with modern science reference geology, not biology (see, e.g. Butler's *Way of All Flesh* or Gosse's *Father and Son*): Darwin's theory was not the challenge or the scandal. Among Baptists, perhaps the most telling example of this is William Bell Riley, among the most significant of the hardline fundamentalist leaders prior to World War II, and organizer, variously, of the World Christian Fundamentals Assocation, the Baptist Bible Union and the General Association of Regular Baptist Churches. In the course of his leadership of Baptist and wider fundamentalist causes, Riley published works straightforwardly denying six-day creationism (most famously the published record of a debate with Harry Rimmer: *A Debate: Resolved, That the Creative Days in Genesis were Aeons, not Solar Days*, in which Riley proposed the motion).

Riley and Rimmer's debate was published 1929, which is somewhat surprising, as the anti-Darwinian mood in the Southern states seems to date from the 1920s. The SBC adopted its confession, Baptist Faith and Message, in 1925, which asserted that 'all sound learning is . . . a part of our Christian heritage'; this was clearly immediately assumed to be a tacit affirmation of evolution, so much so that the day afterwards the Convention passed a resolution denying that BFM affirmed evolution, although remaining carefully silent on the question of the truth or otherwise of Darwinian biology. (The phrase was deleted in the 1963 revision, in which the paragraph on education was completely rewritten to insist, among other things, that 'the freedom of a teacher in a Christian school . . . is limited . . . by the authoritative nature of the Scriptures'; in the 2000 revision, aspects of both the 1925 clause and the 1963 clause were combined, including both of the statements quoted here.) Baptists have been fully involved in the controversy over evolution in the US, but no more so than other evangelicals, and the issue is of less significance in the wider Baptist world (Ernest Lucas, one of the leading public proponents of the compatibility of evolutionary biology and Christian faith in Britain, teaches in a Baptist college, for instance).

Revelation and Theological Method

From the beginning, Baptists have been committed to the authority of Scripture, but this hardly sets them apart from other Christians; perhaps not every Christian theologian has been adequately committed to biblical authority, but those who have were not all Baptists, and the recent theological moves that some have seen as undermining biblical authority have been visible in Baptist life as well as elsewhere. I will be arguing later in this book that there is, in the British Baptist tradition at least, a distinctive way of understanding biblical authority which appears to have lasted through the tradition, but this appears to me to be very geographically limited; at a broader level, Baptists tend to affirm a commitment to biblical authority, but share that with many other Christians.

In the earliest Baptist traditions there were extensive traces of a Separatist 'charismatic' tradition, which disdained prepared sermons or prayers as inevitably quenching the work of the Spirit. At times, it was the practice for the Bible to be closed after the lesson had been read, as even having the text of Scripture available in written form might impair the immediate inspiration of the preacher. Fairly rapidly, however, better theology prevailed in most Baptist contexts. Prior preparation is not a bar to pneumatological inspiration; the Holy Spirit, having the benefit of exhaustive knowledge of past, present and future, can presumably inspire adequately when one prepares on a Wednesday just as much as when one speaks on a Sunday. In their arguments over Calvinism, or missionary methods, or practices of association, or the continuity of the charismata, or the role of men and women in the church, or involvement in ecumenical organizations, Baptists have generally used not just the same theological methods, but often the very same arguments, as other Protestant Christians.

Even at the radical end of the Baptist movement, in Landmarkist and Anti-mission traditions, the arguments used are not very different from those advanced by similar Presbyterian (for example) groups, even if the effect of the argument is sometimes to exclude those others whose method is remarkably similar. The Landmarkist insistence on practising baptism precisely as it was practised in the New Testament, and refusing the validity of all other (supposed) baptism, is exactly equivalent to the 'regulative principle' of conservative Presbyterian worship, under which only that which is explicitly permitted in Scripture may be allowed in Christian worship; that a Baptist reading of Scripture would dismiss conservative Presbyterians as – on the Landmarkist view – not adequately Christian does not alter this fundamental methodological agreement.

Again, the methodological turn to religious experience as justifying theological claims, which has been so significant in academic theology since Schleiermacher, found its exponents in Baptist theology, as we have seen. In the US, for example, Kendrick, Strong and Mullins all explored and employed this methodology; it was determinative for the Chicago School. In Kendrick, the fusing of a Schleiermachian emphasis on religious experience with a natively Baptist interest in revivalism formed a powerful cocktail, but generally the methodological moves these thinkers explored were not distinctively Baptist; the exception perhaps being Mullins's (not entirely successful) attempt to make soul competency the core doctrine out of which all others would naturally arise.

Three twentieth-century writers perhaps deserve mention here, two because their contributions, while not uniquely Baptist, were significant, and one for arguing for a distinctively Baptist (or better baptist) theological method in ways that have been found convincing by many. First, Carl Henry's six-volume *magnum opus God, Revelation, and Authority* offers little or nothing that is specifically Baptist, but stands as perhaps the greatest statement of a contemporary American evangelical tradition that regards biblical inerrancy as the foundational principle of theology, the truth of all doctrine being established on the basis of the claim that God's revelation in Scripture is truthful, adequate and comprehensible. Henry can thus be regarded as a representative – perhaps the most capable representative – of an important contemporary strand of Baptist theology, which finds its identity as part of a broader evangelical tradition, and largely downplays any specifically Baptist distinctives.

The most significant methodological turn in the twentieth century has been the politicization of theology. Beginning with a broadly Marxist analysis of poverty and oppression in a Latin American context, but rapidly spreading to feminist analysis, accounts of the particular history of African Americans and many other marginalized groups, contextual theologies have suggested that all readings of Scripture, and all theological constructions, are decisively affected by the social and political context in which they are done. Traditional theology is not without context, but in fact represents what the gospel looks like from the perspective of a privileged class of white, European, heterosexual males, a class which until recently was the background of almost every academic theologian, and which was arrogant enough to assume its own contextual analysis was in fact universal. Liberation theology, feminist theology, black theology, queer theology and any number of other contextual theologies have been devoted to exposing the oppressive politics which has masqueraded as normal and universal truth in classical theology.

Baptists have not, perhaps, been as assiduous in exploring these contextual traditions as some others; once again, where they have been involved, there has been little attempt to offer explicitly Baptist versions of what has been going on (contextual theologians have in fact tended to be rather uninterested in historical denominational identities; this is not just a Baptist issue). To take only one example, Orlando Costas was perhaps the leading interpreter of Latin American liberation theology within the evangelical tradition, and a Baptist; he was, throughout his life, acutely conscious of the ways in which his experiences and contexts shaped his theological thinking, but never raised his Baptist identity (unlike his evangelical convictions) as a key driver in this. Baptist theologians have not generally found their Baptist identity relevant for their accounts of theological method.

One significant exception, however, is James McClendon (1924–2000), whose three-volume systematic theology, published towards the end of his life, was carefully designed to explore what McClendon regarded as a distinctively Baptist theological methodology. McClendon's formation was within the SBC, although his outspoken political views during the 1960s resulted in him leaving the Baptist academy, and never returning (he was dismissed twice, once from Golden Gate Baptist Seminary for his advocacy of Martin Luther King and the Civil Rights Movement, and then from the University of San Francisco, which has Roman Catholic roots, for his opposition to the Vietnam War). He continued to be active in the broader theological academy, however, and remained extremely conscious of his denominational identity and how that should shape a distinctive theology.

The first volume of his systematics was on *Ethics* (1986), and explored narrative approaches to ethics, proposing non-violence as the centre of a Christian ethical system. McClendon made the claim that, for the believers' church, theology was first lived and then taught, and so a Baptist theology should begin with ethics and move on to doctrine. The second volume, *Doctrine* (1994), proposed a non-foundationalist approach to Christian doctrine, with an ecclesiological and eschatological emphasis; the third volume, *Witness* (2000), offered an account of the interaction of gospel and culture, with the task of the church being to discern where the gospel might be found already in any particular culture, and where the culture must be criticized and challenged on the basis of the gospel. This practice of witness, of confronting the prevailing culture with the claims of the gospel, is the authentic outworking of a Baptistic theology.

McClendon was fascinated with methodological questions, and in evaluating his proposals as a version of specifically Baptist theology, it is important to note that this is not the only concern that shaped his theological method. At least as important was a conviction that theology must move beyond classical foundationalism, the idea that certain ideas are true and basic, and so form a viable foundation for other knowledge. It might be possible to argue for a certain conformity of anti-foundationalism and the idea of a believers' church (both perhaps stand in some relation to the idea that divine revelation is profoundly alien to culturally dominant ways of thinking), but it is certainly not a necessary connection, and so McClendon's methodological proposals should perhaps be seen as *a* Baptist option, not *the* Baptist option.

Conclusion

Demonstrating that Baptist theology is not distinctive on this or that doctrine would be an enormously difficult task and this chapter has not attempted it. Rather, I have tried to show that, where there have been claims for a particular distinctiveness of Baptist theology, they are not historically convincing – even if all Baptists should have thought like this, most Baptists in practice have not. More often, there has been a general acceptance – perhaps even a celebration – among Baptists that, other than on issues of ecclesiology, their theology stands happily in a broader tradition of Protestantism. I have tried to illustrate the plausibility of this assumption in the series of brief examples I have here given. On average, Baptists are perhaps a little more conservative and evangelical than other Protestant groups, but there is nothing distinctive in their theology other than their beliefs about the nature and role of the church, and its officers and sacraments. To these issues, therefore, I now turn.

Chapter 5
The Baptist Vision of the Church

Believer's Baptism

Most Christians in the modern West, if asked what was distinctive about Baptist church life, would probably point to believer's baptism. However, this practice is neither unique to Baptists nor at the heart of their understanding of what it is to be the church. There are areas of the world where believer's baptism is far from a Baptist distinctive: in parts of Latin America, for instance, most of the large Protestant denominations restrict baptism to believers (being Pentecostal in tradition), and so the self-narrated distinctives of the Baptist denominations there can fail to mention baptismal practice at all. Further, it is possible to argue that believer's baptism is an ecumenical Christian practice: faced with a previously unbaptized convert, virtually every Christian denomination would offer baptism (the Salvation Army and the Society of Friends would be the only obvious exceptions); the Baptist distinctive is not in baptizing believers, but in refusing to baptize infants, and in generally refusing to recognize the baptism of infants.

That said, believer's baptism has been a decisive point of identity at various periods in history, and so needs to be considered. The classical Baptist account stresses not just the subject of baptism (one who is already a believer), but its mode (full immersion). I have noted already the unfortunate case of Whitsitt, dismissed from his academic post for making a historically correct observation about the late adoption of the practice of immersion by the seventeenth-century English Baptists; this challenged the mythology that the primitive practice of immersion was preserved by true believers at every point in history and was felt by some to be deeply damaging to Baptist identity. In Britain, there was a significant crisis even earlier, when Baptist supporters of the new Bible Society tried to insist that the Greek work *baptizo* be translated 'immerse' or 'plunge', rather than 'baptize' in Bibles published by the Society. The mode of baptism had become important.

This insistence on immersion highlights a striking feature of historical defences of the Baptist position on baptism: it is far more based on a recovery of biblical praxis than on any reflection on biblical theology. That is, Baptists have tended to argue that the practice of the New Testament church was the immersion of believers only, and so this should be our practice; any consideration of a theology of baptism is seriously subordinated to this demand that New Testament practice be imitated. Baptist writings on baptism rather rarely get beyond this polemical point concerning praxis, arguing far more about the mode (immersion) and subjects (believers only) of baptism than about the meaning and effect of the sacrament/ordinance.[1] Perhaps bizarrely, Baptists have been remarkably poor at developing a theology of baptism over their history, often resting content with developing an account of proper administration of the rite.

One consequence of this has been an inability to engage in ecumenical dialogue. With a conviction that their practice of baptism is biblical, and with no theological account of why this biblical practice is important, or what it achieves, Baptists have often been simply unable to discuss baptism with other Christians. Historically, this has resulted in two conflicting positions: a hard line, 'this is biblical, there is no room for discussion, what you do is wrong' position; and a much softer 'we believe this is biblical, we recognize that you do not, we lack the language to explore the dispute, so we will try to find a pragmatic way of coexisting' position. The former position, found most purely in the Landmarkist tradition, is probably more characteristic of American Baptist life, and is more generally the case around the Baptist world; the latter is more commonly found in British Baptist traditions, and also in parts of Europe (such as Sweden) and in South Australia.

Very few American Baptist churches at any point in history would regard questions of an open communion table and open membership as live and interesting issues. ('Open' here means available to those not baptized as believers.) To be Baptist is to be committed to the baptism of believers only, and to the restriction of both the communion table and membership of the church to true Christians, which means those baptized as believers. The Landmarkist tradition is unquestionably the far edge of American Baptist witness, but on this issue it represents the striking conservatism of the mainstream. (The most high-profile advocate of the open communion position in America is generally agreed to be Benjamin Randal, the founder of the Freewill Baptist Connexion; that no prominent Calvinist defender can be found demonstrates the marginal nature of the position.) There was a brief flirtation with open membership among some Northern churches around the beginning of the twentieth century; in 1925 the Northern Convention meeting was invited to exclude such churches; while it did not in fact do so, a resolution passed in 1926 was at least deeply discouraging of the open membership position, and in fact excluded anyone not baptized by immersion as a believer from participation in convention meetings. This slightly weaker formulation has as much to do with the Convention not being prepared to dictate policy to local churches as with any lack of conviction that the open membership position was simply wrong.

British Baptists, by contrast, have repeatedly located themselves within broader movements, and so have been much more open to non-Baptists within their fellowships and at their communion tables. In the seventeenth century, Baptists often retained fraternal relationships with those Separatist churches which had given them birth – as in the various splits and reunions around the Jacob-Lanthrop-Jessey congregation in London – and so were not always prepared to unchurch those whose baptismal practice was different. Mixed congregations of Baptists and non-Baptist Separatists were not uncommon (the later years of Jessey's congregation, and John Bunyan's church, would be the two most high-profile examples). This was no doubt strengthened by Baptists making political, and military, common cause with other radical Protestants in the Civil War. Following the Restoration, the context of persecution led to Baptists working with other Dissenters to seek liberty of worship in law in England. The famous (and still existing) Deputies of the Three Dissenting Denominations originated in an ecumenical meeting of Baptists, Congregationalists and Presbyterians in 1732. Congregations from the three denominations within ten miles of London were to elect 'deputies' who would press for the repeal of the Test and Corporation Acts. The first recorded meeting of the Deputies is in 1737.

Later, shared evangelical convictions seemed more important than denominational distinctives to many Baptists, and Baptists are fully represented in the founding of the pan-evangelical bodies of the early nineteenth century, including the Bible Society, the London Missionary Society, the anti-slavery societies and many others. There was a deliberate decision in this early phase of pan-evangelicalism to put ecclesiological disagreements to one side in order to promote agreement over the gospel. There were, of course, tensions: disputes that threatened the work of the Bible Society have already been noted, and as soon as the LMS found enough success to imagine starting a congregation, the impracticality of its original charter, which demanded it held no position on baptism or church order, became very evident...

Individual Baptist congregations have negotiated the ecumenical question in different ways. From the origins of the Particular Baptist movement, in the Jacob-Lathrop-Jessey church and its offshoots, there was a degree of charity. As noted above, as significant a figure as John Bunyan was pastor of a mixed church, which practised both believer's baptism and infant baptism. At the turn of the eighteenth century, perhaps as a result of pan-evangelical mobility, the question of allowing non-baptized believers to the communion table became pressing. Through the contributions of Robert Hall of Leicester, in particular his celebrated *On the Terms of Communion* (1815), the 'open communion' tradition became normal, if far from universal, in Britain; in recent years it has gained some ground elsewhere in Europe also. The question of 'open' membership – the practice of allowing non-baptized believers formally to become members of the church upon profession of faith – has lasted longer, not least for legal reasons: English Baptist churches are legally established through trust deeds, which specify their objects, and the conditions for membership. If 'closed' membership is written in to the trust deed, there has until recently been little possibility of change. The sentiments that prevailed when a church was founded are therefore decisive; around London in particular, there are many churches established on closed-membership principles because of the influence of Spurgeon (who practised open communion, but closed membership).

British Baptists find themselves in a curious position as a result of this tradition of ecumenical openness: they are, in practice, less committed to the importance of baptism in ecclesiology than almost any other mainstream denomination. In most British Baptist churches a person may be in membership or even leadership, and may receive or even celebrate the Eucharist, without being baptized, either as believer or infant. No other British denomination (excluding the Salvation Army, of course) is as lax in its baptismal polity as the main line Baptists. In recent years there has been a reaction to this, with an increasing number of Baptist scholars arguing for the importance, and the power, of baptism on exegetical and theological grounds, but often seeking to find ways of recognizing infant baptism (when coupled with some form of personal profession of faith) as efficacious and so valid, even if improper.

This cautious openness to some form of infant baptism found institutional recognition in 2005, when the Baptist Union of Great Britain and the Church of England jointly published a report of ecumenical conversations. The report, entitled 'Pushing at the Boundaries of Unity', invited Baptist congregations to reflect on whether 'they might recognize a place for the baptism of infants within the whole journey that marks the beginning of the Christian life', and challenged the practice of asking for 're-baptism' of those who had been baptized as infants.[2] In 2006, the Council of the Baptist Union of Great Britain declined to 'welcome' this report, but agreed to 'accept' it, and to refer it for further study by member churches. Very recently, some study material based on the report has been published by BUGB.

Two broad theological understandings of baptism can be discerned through Baptist history, which I will term 'symbolic' and 'sacramental'. The symbolic tradition, so much in the ascendancy that it went unquestioned until relatively recently, asserts that baptism (like the Eucharist) is an enacted sermon: such power as it has is in the narration and display of the gospel story. It is important because commanded by Jesus, but nothing special happens when a person is baptized. Baptism is an act of witness and obedience, and the personal testimony of the baptismal candidates to the workings of grace in their lives, and their enacted obedience to the instruction of Jesus, form the core of the rite. Some recent writers, drawn from across the Baptist world, have suggested an alternative understanding, which they claim is both more adequate theologically and exegetically, and has deep roots within the Baptist tradition. Core to this view would be a belief that the fact of being baptized changes something about a person. Baptism on this sacramental understanding is a 'means of grace', an act which is accompanied by a promise that the Holy Spirit will be at work in and through this act.

A combination of causes has led to the attractiveness of this new view. First, there seems to be a strong exegetical basis for believing that baptism is more than a mere symbol. George Beasley-Murray's masterful study *Baptism in the New Testament* is of crucial importance here,[3] both for arguing the position compellingly, and because Beasley-Murray was so widely respected in the Baptist world that his view carried significant personal authority. A succession of later scholars continued to argue the exegetical point, however, and it might now be regarded as well established. Second, there is a striking convergence of sacramental theology and charismatic renewal in Baptist life in Europe and America, coupled with a similar openness to more supernaturalist ways of understanding theology in the churches of the global South. Clearly, a spirituality that is generally open to and expectant of supernatural acts of God in the life of the church makes it easier to believe that the Spirit is at work in the context of baptism.[4] Third, Baptist involvement in ecumenical dialogue has led to repeated exposure to other, generally more sacramental, ways of understanding baptism; exposure like this does not guarantee agreement, of course, but it does allow consideration of a broader range of positions. Fourth, those championing the new developments suggest that historical study of the beliefs of early Baptists support their contentions.[5] Their telling of the history would deny (correctly, in my estimation) that their view is novel among Baptists; rather they would insist that a belief that God is active to change the one baptized in the act of baptism has been normal, being assumed by all Baptists until about 1800, but then supplanted by an alien view for the next hundred and fifty years or so. The espousal of a sacramental view is, on this telling, a return to the tradition, not a departure from it.

The practice of believer's baptism coheres theologically with other Baptist distinctives, which I shall explore later, such as religious liberty (see Chapter 6), a focus on mission (see Chapter 7) and a call to visible holiness on the part of every Christian (see again Chapter 7). In Baptist theology, God deals directly with each particular human being, summoning him or her to respond in repentance and faith to the gospel call, and to take his or her place within the active community of the redeemed, living a life of visible holiness and committed to the evangelization of the world. Believer's baptism is an expression of this intensely individualist strain within Baptist theology: the faith of the church or the family is of no moment in the story of a person's journey to faith; only his or her own response counts, and so baptism comes at his or her request, and not as a result of some proxy decision.

(The word 'individual' has received some criticism in recent theology; the roots of this are in John Zizioulas's *Being as Communion*, which represents (infant) baptism as the sacrament in which God deconstructs our sinful individuality, and re-makes us as persons, constituted by our connections to other persons in the church.[6] I have written elsewhere about my questions concerning Zizioulas's proposed ontology of personhood; here I simply observe that his claim that it is only our baptismal relatedness to the institutional church that enables our relatedness to God is precisely what the practice of believer's baptism opposes. Baptists believe that God addresses, calls and saves human beings as individuals; we do not need to be ashamed of that.)

The Primacy of the Local Church

Alongside this individualist strand of Baptist belief is a very strong commitment to the importance of the local church. God's call comes to individuals, it is true, but the call is to become a part of a community of faith. Baptism is ordinarily accompanied by reception into membership of a particular local church; immersion into the gathered community is the inevitable result of immersion into the water. Alongside believer's baptism, then, the other major ecclesiological distinctive shared by Baptists is congregational church government. This is the doctrine that the church is formed and led by mutual agreement of all of its members. It does not need outside authorization (as from Bishop or presbytery) to be a true church of Christ, nor does it cede control of its own affairs to a priest or a group of elders. I will discuss congregational government in more detail later in this chapter; for now the primacy of the local church will be the focus of attention.

Once again, the most militant version of this can be found in nineteenth-century America, and the birth of the Primitive Baptists in the anti-missions movement. The Primitives operated with a regulative principle which insisted that, at least in the sphere of ecclesial practice, nothing not explicitly commanded in the New Testament was permissible. The only form of Christian organization they could find in the New Testament was the local church, so no other formal organization was acceptable. This was true of organizations within churches – there was no place for an organized women's meeting, for instance – and of parachurch organizations, such as missions societies or Bible societies. Primitive Baptist churches would join together in quasi-denominational structures, but they were always organized to stress the primary place of the local congregation, and in particular to prevent any transfer of power from the local churches to the wider body. For example, when seventeen anti-mission churches withdrew from the Alabama Convention in 1838, they did not become independent churches, but immediately founded a new association of their own, which enshrined their principles in its terms of association (it was called the Ebenezer Association).

All Baptists, however, are committed to both the independence, and the primacy, of the local church. Churches commit to membership of various bodies, but may always voluntarily withdraw from them, and regularly do; within Baptist polity, no denominational decision can commit a church to any doctrinal or ethical decision. (My own experience of this includes serving on bilateral ecumenical conversations as the representative of a Baptist denomination; at one point, fairly late on, our partners from the other tradition finally grasped the centrality of our Baptist convictions concerning the local church, and asked what power a Baptist denomination had to instruct its churches to recognize the ministry or faith of another denomination; our response, that the only power available was moral suasion, and that local congregations would be free to ignore the decision of the central body, was met with equal parts of exasperation and incredulity.) A denomination may, of course, adopt or vary a confession of faith, including on doctrinal matters (so, historically, many Baptist denominations have taken a definite line on predestination, for instance), but this decision cannot be imposed on any church. At most, the local congregation might be excluded from the denomination.

The primacy of the local church in Baptist understanding is best exemplified by the unusual Baptist use of the word 'church'. There is no 'Baptist church' that is not a local congregation: associations, conventions and unions are just that – associations and conventions and unions of local churches. Baptists acknowledge, of course, the unity of the universal church of Christ, but that universal church is only instantiated in local congregations; for Baptists, language of the 'Presbyterian Church of the US' or the 'Church of South India' or the 'Methodist Church' is both meaningless and dangerously distracting: a church is a body that gathers together for worship (including the administration of baptism and the celebration of the Eucharist), mutual edification and discipline, and to discern the mind of Christ for its life; an organization that cannot gather like this cannot be a church. (The church universal is precisely the body that will be gathered by Christ on the last day, when the dead rise, and so is not an exception to this principle.)

Baptists would claim that in this they represent authentic apostolic practice. In particular, in response to the repeated ecumenical emphasis on the importance for the unity of the church of the 'sign' of episcopacy,[7] Baptists would want to point to the origins of this sign: the unity of the church was preserved because in each place there was one bishop, serving one congregation, celebrating one Eucharist (and because the bishops were in fellowship with one another); a church, in patristic and Baptist understanding, is a group that meets to break bread in memory of the death of the Lord Jesus, and in expectation of his return; any organization that cannot do this may be useful and appropriate, but it is not a church, and so it is not necessary to God's purposes, and is of (at best) secondary importance ecclesiologically.

This does not mean that Baptists would deny the creedal claim that the church is marked by unity, apostolicity, sanctity and catholicity ('I believe in one, holy, catholic and apostolic church'). While the Nicene Creed has not been a primary point of reference for Baptists over history, their appeal being always to Scripture alone,[8] it is difficult to find any criticism of the text. This is unsurprising: Baptists have, necessarily, been at pains to profess their Christian orthodoxy in the face of suspicious authorities through much of their history, and any attack on the Nicene Creed would have been taken as compelling evidence of heresy.[9] Generally, Baptists have been more vocal concerning the Reformation marks of the true church (the pure preaching of the Word, the right administration of the sacraments and the exercise of church discipline) than in the Nicene marks. The Nicene marks have become central for ecumenical theology in the twentieth century, however, and so Baptists have found themselves having to negotiate them. Like every other Christian tradition, Baptists have interpreted these marks according to their own ecclesiology.

Baptists believe straightforwardly in the unity of the church: Christ has one church, composed of all true believers from all times and places. Baptists would be very suspicious, indeed disdainful, of any attempt to identify this one church with any particular historical organization (including their own). A local church, gathered together to hear the Word preached, administering the dominical sacraments of baptism and Eucharist, and covenanted to watch over one another's walk, is the proper visible instantiation of this one church. Belief in the unity of the church has at least one important practical outworking for Baptists, though: the historic commitment to the association of true Christian churches. I will have more to say about this in a moment.

Arguments over the meaning of the apostolicity of the church have often followed the historic Reformation divisions: for the Roman Catholic Church, the primary mark of apostolicity is the continuity of the institutional church, founded by the apostles on Christ's instruction. Bishops are the successors of the apostles, charged with, and gifted by, the Holy Spirit for the continuance of the apostolic teaching and mission, and so the continuity of the episcopate within the church renders the church apostolic. By contrast, the Reformation churches, both Lutheran and Reformed, stressed the conformity with apostolic teaching as the mark of being truly apostolic. They claimed that the Church of Rome had erred and departed from the apostolic teaching and so was no longer truly apostolic; their recovery of New Testament Christianity, the teaching of the apostles, was a return to true apostolicity. If forced to choose between these two, Baptists would generally be happier with the latter position (although Landmarkist claims concerning the historical continuity of true Baptist churches could be seen as a version of the former, Catholic, position). Some Baptists have, however, begun to claim a third account, seeing participation in the apostolic mission as central to claiming to be apostolic.

The primary role of the apostles, on this account, was to make disciples (Mt. 28.19). 'Apostle' means, very simply, 'one sent', and Christ's apostles are sent to turn people into followers of Jesus. Teaching what the apostles taught, and the establishment, organization and maintenance of churches, are alike only means to that end. (In Mt. 28, 'teaching' and 'baptizing' are grammatically subordinate to 'making disciples' – the way that primary aim is to be accomplished.) For the church to be 'apostolic', therefore, is for it to be about the business of making new disciples of Christ; a church that is actively involved in the evangelization of the world is apostolic, and so a true church; a church which is not is failing fundamentally in its calling.

Now, these different positions can be read as matters of emphasis, rather than as exclusive options. The present *Catholic Catechism* notes the transmission of apostolic teaching and the continuance of the apostolic mission as part of what it is to be apostolic, but subsumes them under the basic head of the role of the bishops as successors to the apostles. Baptists would certainly not deny that careful attention to biblical teaching is important, and have generally been very conscious of the need to recognize their place in the history of God's people – Robert Robinson, writing the history of the congregation he pastored in Cambridge (England), begins his account with the sons of Noah! Stressing the missional nature of apostolicity, however, seems to capture something of the biblicist nature of Baptist exegesis and to locate the call to spread the gospel in the very DNA of the church, which captures a historic Baptist emphasis well. I will say more about this in Chapter 7.

The holiness of the church has often been understood 'positionally'; that is, the church is holy because set apart for God, not because of any particular ethical perfection. This, historically, is a response to the reality of mass Christianity and state churches, and the creation of Christian communities which chose not to police their ethical boundaries with any particular energy. For Baptists, while they would not deny the positional holiness of the church, there is a need for a visible holiness also, which manifests itself in two ways. First, Baptist churches are believers' churches, requiring a profession of faith in Christ, and a commitment to follow him, of every member. Second, the practice of church discipline maintains the holiness of the church by requiring true repentance of anyone who commits visible sin and excluding the unrepentant. Again, I will have much more to say about this in Chapter 7.

Finally, the catholicity of the church is a claim concerning universality. The church is not limited to a particular culture or locality, but exists in all places. For Baptists, this would be seen as a critique of the practice of state churches, which over-identify with particular cultures. The Christian's primary loyalty is to the church catholic, not to his or her own community or nation. Roman Catholic accounts of the catholicity of the church have seen a call to mission in this claim: because the church should exist in all cultures and places, there is a need to plant churches in places where they do not currently exist. I am not aware of any Baptist borrowing of this idea, but it would fit well with a Baptist insistence on the missional essence of the local church. I will have more to say about Baptist commitment to a practical catholicity at the end of the next section (on church government).

Congregational Church Government

In Baptist practice, the local church is governed by the church meeting, when all members gather to seek together the mind of Christ. Church meeting has been a remarkably varied practice through history: formal mechanisms for decision-making vary from a requirement to find consensus through the following of

Robert's Rules (which codify parliamentary procedure and guide the running of formal meetings of all sorts) to varieties of secret ballot, possibly including postal voting. Agendas vary from a focus on policing the behaviour of members of the church to a concentration on managing the assets of the church, both finance and fabric. Frequency and timing vary widely; historically some churches restricted formal participation to male members only. In some contexts, the church meeting does little more than appoint officers (typically elders and deacons) who then, in practice, run the church. Given all this variation, why do Baptists place such emphasis on the church meeting as a defining part of their identity?

The primary doctrine of the church among Baptists is a stress on the Lordship of Christ. Of course, all Christian denominations will claim this; the Baptist distinctive is applying this resolutely to the local congregation. Polemically, this gives rise to the insistence on the primacy of the local congregation already discussed: anyone, king, magistrate, pope or bishop who seeks to control the local gathered church is, on a classical Baptist understanding, simply and precisely usurping the place of Christ. In terms of positive polity, this teaching raises a question: how is Christ's Lordship experienced or known in the local church? It would be possible to point to a particular congregational leader, or a group of leaders, who are believed to have particular insight into Christ's will for the congregation; Baptists have traditionally resisted this. All the members of the local church are corporately responsible for discerning the mind of Christ for that people. Church meeting, however practised, is the organizational expression of this belief.

Whence the belief? I have noted already that the practice of believers' baptism gives rise to a certain sort of individualism in Baptist ecclesiology. Christ deals directly, or perhaps mediately, through the Holy Spirit, with every particular believer. From this claim it is an easy step to insist that every particular believer in a given fellowship should be involved in the discerning of Christ's call on the fellowship, and so in the governance of the church. In recent years it has been easy to conflate the belief with modern Western individualism, and the practice with democracy,[10] and so to see Baptist polity as merely aping or echoing the culture of the day. Baptist commitments to such positions pre-date contemporary democratic structures by many decades, however, and more often served as prophetic protests in favour of recognizing the intrinsic worth of every human being, rather than as mirrors of what was current in culture.

The first manual on Baptist church order to commend balloting as good procedure was Charles Stovel's *Hints on the regulation of Christian churches . . .* published in England in 1835; in 1832, the Reform Act had been passed, extending the franchise in England to about 650,000 men, or about 10 per cent of the male population. Stovel thus takes a cultural practice which is available only to a cultural elite of male property owners, and puts it in the hands of all believers, male and female, regardless of their social class or economic situation. This was no passive aping of contemporary political mores; rather it was a profoundly subversive remodelling. (The practice of only allowing male members to vote, known mainly in the second half the seventeenth century in a few British Baptist churches, seems to be an implicit recognition of, and revulsion at, this basic egalitarianism implied in the practice of church meeting.)

The practice of church meeting is not democratic, secondly, because the task of all present is not to express a preference, still less to gain a majority, but to discern together the mind of Christ. The church gathers corporately to seek to hear its Lord's voice and to commit itself to obey what it has heard. Where it is practised, the insistence on finding consensus in church meeting reflects this: church members are called to submit themselves to the will of Christ, not to indicate their own preferences or desires. That said, this consensual practice is fairly rare among Baptists (Quakers and some Anabaptist groups would be more often committed to something like this), perhaps because of a healthy dose of Augustinian realism about the lack of growth in holiness of at least some church members. In this or that area, one or another member may be deaf to the call of Christ, and so a majority is acceptable.

As noted in passing above, some Baptist traditions permit postal or proxy voting by members on key decisions; in straightforwardly democratic terms, the logic of this is impeccable, so much so that resistance to it demands explanation; where it is resisted, it is because of an awareness that the task of church meeting is knowing the mind of Christ, and a sense that this can only be done in the gathered body. Again, Baptist practices, when interrogated, make it clear that the basic impetus is not a belief in democracy, but a belief that it is the corporate responsibility of all to discern the mind of Christ.

This account of the theological importance of the practice of church meeting for Baptists is perhaps most vulnerable to the observation of widely varying agendas across time and tradition. In the British Baptist tradition, for instance, church meetings prior to circa 1800 were almost always focused on policing the Christian conduct of members, whereas by 1900, and down to the present day, agendas will more typically be focused, at least in large part, on financial and fabric issues. Has Christ changed his mind about what matters in his churches?

The answer, of course, is more that the churches have changed their minds about, in some cases what is primary to being church, and in other cases how to fulfil Christ's calling. Almost all British Baptist churches would still take seriously the need to watch over the behaviour of fellow members, but much of the informal encouragement and rebuke that was previously done in church meeting would now be done quietly by those to whom the low-level pastoral tasks of the church have been assigned, typically pastors and elders. (Excommunication is still a matter for the church meeting; in practice, in contemporary Britain, a member is very likely to disassociate him- or herself from the church, and probably to find a welcome in a different local fellowship, long before the point of a formal consideration at church meeting is reached.)

The twentieth-century focus on matters of fabric can perhaps best be read as part of a concern for mission. Around the beginning of the twentieth century many urban and suburban Baptist churches found that mission through a variety, in some cases a plethora, of community organizations – youth clubs, sports clubs, women's meetings and so forth – was effective. The maintenance of such a programme of mission, however, demanded the upkeep of an extensive church plant, and so a degree of focus on fabric matters. (If this analysis is correct, then we might expect to see matters of fabric dropping off church meeting agendas slowly, at least in Britain and America, as the contemporary emphasis on mission among Baptists in those countries is far more of the 'church without walls' variety.)

One final comment about the practice of church meeting is worth making, returning to the catholicity of the church discussed briefly above. It has sometimes been difficult, operating at the level of doctrinal abstraction, for Baptists to give an account of how their commitment to (a measure of) catholicity works out in their ecclesiology. If each local congregation governs itself, without intervention from the wider church, how can Baptist churches reflect the riches of whatever broader Christian church they recognize (and even in the extreme case of Landmarkist sectarianism, at least other Landmarkist churches are recognized, and so there is some small measure of catholicity to be expressed). The actual practice of church meeting, however, makes a measure of informal but real catholicity obvious, as in the course of their discussions members will bring insights borrowed from other Christians they have read or talked to, from conferences they have attended, from other fellowships they have been part of and so on, as well as perhaps the leadership bringing insight from consulting other fellowships or denominational bodies, and/or those with a measure of formal theological training bringing knowledge from their studies to bear.

The Independence and Interdependence of Local Churches

This question of practical catholicity of a Baptist church suggests that the next issue to be considered is the interdependence of local churches, or 'associationalism', as it is known in Baptist life. As stated above, the principle of the independence of the local church is the claim that a particular congregation needs nothing beyond itself to be a true church of Christ; that does not mean that it is free to ignore whatever lies beyond the bounds of its own fellowship. Instead, Baptists have, virtually from their foundation, held that true churches have a duty to unite together for support and instruction. The most famous statement of this imperative is unquestionably the founding minute of the Abingdon Association, written in October 1652:

> That perticular churches of Christ ought to hold firme communion each with other in point of advice in doubtful matters and controversies . . . because there is the same

> relation betwixt the perticular churches each towards other as there is betwixt perticular members of one church.[11]

Given the importance for Baptist accounts of discipleship of the local church, particularly of the act of covenanting together to watch over one another, this is a remarkably strong statement. There is, on this account, both a theological duty for churches to associate and a need for them to associate for their own growth and good health. While association has not been a universal Baptist practice (there are everywhere a small number of independent churches, unassociated with any other), Smith's claim that 'it is demonstrably true that the Baptist association, as an institution, has given continuity to the Baptist movement for more than three centuries' is generally justified, and not just in America (the context he was describing in writing the comment).[12]

The universality of associating does not imply a uniformity of practice. Churches come together to support and help one another; the expectations and limits placed upon the association, the patterns of meeting, the selection of delegates – all are practices almost endlessly varied in Baptist life. To offer only one example, I have already noted controversies over the extent of associational power to form mission societies and the like. It is worth repeating, however, that anti-mission churches, even at the moment they are most virulently opposed to attacks on their autonomy, and so are withdrawing from their former associations, almost invariably tended to form or join new associations that more adequately upheld their views (as in the example of the founding of the Ebenezer Association in Alabama, noted above). Baptist churches seem to believe that they belong together, not apart, and to act on that belief.

I am not especially interested here in the varying organizational principles of associations, although these have been important historically (at least a part of the sectional controversy, leading to the split of the Southern Baptist Convention from the Northern churches, was over tensions concerning different preferred modes of organizing associational life). My focus must be on the theology that underpins every mode of organization, and in disputes such as the sectional controversy, there is little debate or disagreement about the underlying theology. The Abingdon doctrine gives us a way of reflecting on that theology. Most Baptists would agree that a Christian believer who finds him- or herself deprived of any Christian fellowship is in an uncomfortable place, but not an impossible one. Christian fellowship, paradigmatically expressed in church membership, is a great benefit to Christian discipleship, and should certainly never be wilfully withdrawn from or spurned, but in the extreme case (shipwreck on a desert island? In Baptist history, solitary confinement by persecuting authorities has been the more pertinent, if generally less permanent, example) the lone believer's faith is not rendered impossible by his or her aloneness. Just so, the Christian church, which finds no other true church with which to have fellowship, can exist as a church; the repeated incidences of 'self-baptism' among Baptist pioneers in various contexts suggests that they repeatedly felt themselves to be in such a place. However, where fellowship with other true churches is possible, then it is both a duty and a benefit to enter into it. (And those who self-baptized often later repented of the practice when they discovered that there were in fact churches they could recognize as truly Christian, even if they had previously been unaware of them.)

The benefit of association can be explained by reflecting on the catholicity of the church, as discussed above. In the context of a difficult and acrimonious congregational dispute, perhaps, a fellow congregation might offer disinterested, and so perceptive, advice, or might have struggled with similar questions and so have counsel to offer. Certainly the records of associational life are full of queries from local churches about what to think about this, or how to act concerning that. Sometimes the association has a ready answer, having met the question before; more often it serves as a context in which members of several congregations can pool their insights and resources to generate new wisdom to pass on. (The advice thus gathered can never be binding on the church that raised the question, of course, but has usually been received with gratitude and acceptance.) Continuing this theme of catholicity, an association can also represent the wider church in the life of the local congregation. It is common Baptist practice to invite other local pastors to share in a service of ordination or induction of a new pastor, for instance; not because the congregation is not competent to ordain its own ministry, but because it is appropriate that, if it can, it opens such central and formative acts to receive the prayers and approval of the wider fellowship of Christ's church.

Beyond this, and beginning to stray into the territory that was found controversial in mid-nineteenth-century America, an association can offer local churches the ability to do things they could not do alone. Perhaps most commonly in Baptist life, associations of churches acted together to found institutions for the training of ministers and other workers. While the earliest training institutions tended to be founded through the vision and energy of an individual pastor and church (as Bristol Baptist Academy, the earliest denominational institution, was), and this pattern never wholly disappeared (Spurgeon's Pastor's College in the mid-nineteenth century; examples of similar proposals are not difficult to discover in Baptist life today). Generally, however, the founding – and certainly the later maintenance – of an educational institution has been a task churches have cooperated in, often through existing associational structures. Associations have sometimes been conduits of missionaries and financial support for missions; more often in Baptist life foreign missions, in particular, have been the provenance of mission societies, separated from associational structures, although of course drawing on the same churches and as often as not relying on the very same volunteers for their upkeep. However, mission societies are also a product of the impulse to associationalism: churches choose to band together to further their mission and ministry.

One striking feature of a Baptist doctrine of association is the ease with which it transfers to the contemporary ecumenical arena. I have already commented on the willingness of British Baptists, in particular, to make common cause, even to the extent of shared membership of organizations, with other churches, first other Dissenters, and later other evangelicals. This can be seen as a further outworking of the basic associational theological impulse: to the extent that a non-Baptist fellowship can be recognized as a genuine, if imperfect, church of Christ, there is a positive duty for the Baptist church making that recognition to act on it, to form a relationship of mutual edification and support with the non-Baptist fellowship.

Understood like this, it will be obvious that a Baptist ecumenism will look rather different from the general practices of the ecumenical movement (in which, however, at least some Baptists and Baptist denominations participate). A Baptist ecumenism would be built on growing and organic relationships of understanding and trust between particular local congregations that are able to recognize one another as true gospel churches, leading to shared worship and mission. National and international bodies working at the level of reconciling ancient confessional differences could be an important aid or spur to the formation or furtherance of such local arrangements (more often for Baptists they might be an attempt to formalize already-existing local realities), but are not the primary vehicle for ecumenism.

The Word of God; the Spirit of God

The centrality of the Bible to Baptist ecclesiology will already be evident; this finds practical expression in the centrality of preaching within Baptist worship. This centrality is already evident in the seventeenth century – the 1644 London Confession, for instance, noted (Art. XLV) that some are to 'prophesie . . . to teach publickly the Word of God, for the edification, exhortation, and comfort of the Church'. Of course, Baptists were hardly unique among Protestant traditions in this stated stress on preaching; however, the relative importance for Baptists might be illustrated by noting that preaching is mentioned in six Articles of the confession, whereas the Eucharist is not mentioned directly at all (Art. XXXIII speaks of the '[o]rdinances commanded by Christ,' a reference to Baptism and Eucharist; Baptism is later discussed, of course, but the Eucharist is nowhere else mentioned). Most Baptist acts of worship will be non-Eucharistic: while traditions vary widely, and some churches will celebrate the Eucharist every week (Spurgeon would be the most famous defender of this practice), a monthly celebration is probably most common. It is much more difficult to find a Baptist service of worship where there is no sermon preached.

Equally, the most honoured Baptist leaders are generally the great preachers: from Bunyan and Keach through Spurgeon and Fosdick to Billy Graham, most leaders who have risen to lasting prominence in the movement have built their reputation in large part on a preaching ministry. Baptist worship almost universally lacks a fixed liturgy, or any recitation of creedal statements; in this context, the sermon almost inevitably assumes a centrality in expressing and defining the faith of the church, and in expressing and modelling an authentically Christian response to issues or events that are significant in the life of the church and community. This can sometimes be challenged by a developed liturgical practice, but, in general, it is not unreasonable, however, to assert that across the world and across history, the sermon has been the central focus of Baptist worship.

Liturgical practices beyond the sermon have varied for Baptists. In the first century of the movement, an argument over the propriety of singing hymns, as opposed to just metrical psalms, was decisively won by Benjamin Keach (remarkably, given the sheer awfulness of many of Keach's published hymns), and some practice of congregational singing has remained the norm. Where the liturgy has become more significant, it has generally been as a result of a Baptist adoption of a broader development in Christian worship. In recent years, for instance, we might think of the liturgical movement of the mid-twentieth century, which was less influential among Baptists than almost any other tradition, but nonetheless shaped the worship of some fellowships in significant ways, leading to a new attention to the construction of the liturgy and a new importance accorded to the Eucharist. Charismatic renewal, and the tradition of contemporary worship more broadly, has been far more influential, and has affected many churches, leading to a new emphasis on extended times of sung worship within the service. Most recently, perhaps, 'seeker-sensitive' worship, a model developed by Willow Creek Community Church near Chicago, has been adopted for at least some services by Baptist churches in various parts of the world. In this model performance – solo or choir singing, drama, dance and so forth – assumes significant importance as being (perceived to be) more accessible to outsiders who are being aggressively invited to attend the services.

Patterns of Baptist preaching have varied across the centuries, of course, just as wider Christian traditions of preaching have. It is probable that Baptists have generally been more hospitable to more narrowly expositional preaching than to broader discursive modes, but the example of Fosdick demonstrates that this tendency cannot be elevated into a principle. One curious pattern found in early Baptist preaching provides a useful transition to my next theme, although it rapidly died out. In Helwys's congregation, and some other early congregations, the understanding of preaching as 'prophesying' led to a conviction that preaching should be immediately inspired by the Holy Spirit, and so that the preacher should not rely on prepared notes (or even, in some versions, an open Bible; after the reading of the text, the Bible would be shut ceremonially to ensure the preacher relied only on inspiration). It is no doubt a good thing for the general quality of Baptist preaching that this practice rapidly died out (Baptists, in common with other radical Protestant groups, remained suspicious of prayers that were not delivered extempore), but it points to a charismatic focus in Baptist worship: the immediate work of the Spirit is something that Baptists have traditionally expected and looked for when gathered together.

In recent years, some Baptists have been open and welcoming of the charismatic movement, of course; this is not my primary interest here, however. The distinctive teaching of the contemporary charismatic movement, as of its Pentecostal precursor, is not the present reality of the action of the Holy Spirit, but that certain 'supernatural' gifts, long regarded by mainstream Christians as withdrawn from the church, are in fact still given by the Spirit, and so church fellowships should expect healing miracles, miraculous knowledge (through prophecy, visions, or dreams) and prayer in tongues, with interpretation following, to be a normal part of their experience of worship. Baptists, in common with adherents of most other Christian traditions, can disagree about this teaching; their tradition, however, supposes the present action of the Holy Spirit to be a central part of the life of the local church.

For Baptists, as already indicated, the local church is under the direct rule of Christ. Christ's will is known in the church through shared reflection on Scripture, guided the Spirit's inspiration (as a Russian Baptist confession has it, 'Every church has as its only head Jesus Christ and is administered by His Word and through the guidance of the Holy Spirit through prayer and communion at gatherings'[13]). Baptist polity, therefore simply assumes ongoing pneumatological inspiration within the local church. This is not unregulated: the Spirit does not inspire just anything, but interpretations and applications of the Word. Nonetheless, it is a famous Baptist confession that God has more light and truth to bring forth from Scripture; more significantly, perhaps, the way Scripture is to be heard speaking to a particular local pastoral or missional situation cannot be predicted in advance, determined by association or denomination or known certainly by leaders within the congregation. The mind of Christ is given by the Spirit to the gathered people within the local church. On a Baptist view, therefore, authority rests in Christ alone, but because Christ's will is discerned in the church meeting, authority derivatively rests with all the members of the church corporately.

Leadership within the Church

This of course raises the question of church leadership. Baptists have generally in their history held that God calls and gifts leaders for each local congregation, and that the life of the congregation is incomplete without such leaders. Recognized leadership is of the *bene esse* of the local church, if not of its *esse*. The general, but by no means universal, Baptist pattern of leadership is twofold: elders and deacons, whose responsibilities are respectively for the spiritual guidance and practical care of the church. Most Baptist traditions practice ordination, although their understanding of the rite differs substantially; typically, the ordained minister takes the role of an elder in the church, either the sole elder, or as a member of a team, or 'court' of elders.

Ordination, in most Baptist understandings, confers no special abilities on the one ordained. He or she is not uniquely able to celebrate the Eucharist, to preach the Word or to perform any other task. Normally an ordained minister will take the lead in these roles in his or her own church, but in the absence of the minister, another may serve, and even in the presence of the minister, it would not be unusual in many Baptist traditions for someone else to preach and to celebrate the Eucharist from time to time. What, then, is ordination in Baptist understanding?

An adequately theological answer to that question must begin with baptism. In baptism, the disciple is committed to the service of Christ in the church and the world. There is an important sense in which all Baptists are 'ordained': even under the ecumenical definition proposed in the important World Council of Churches document, *Baptism, Eucharist and Ministry*, the practice of baptism in Baptist churches would seem to fulfil all the requirements for the setting apart of ordained ministers. (The document speaks of ministers as those 'who have received a charism and whom the church appoints for service by ordination through the invocation of the Spirit and the laying on of hands'.[14]) In a recent Baptist slogan, Baptist ecclesiology is not anti-clerical; it is rather 'the abolition of the laity'. Any Baptist account of ordination must begin with this fundamental orientation.

Further, within the local church deacons and lay elders (if the church has them) will also be set aside for service by prayer and the laying on of hands, their gifting having been recognized (so to, often enough, will those who work with children and young people and others). A Baptist account of ordained ministry must either deny its significance, or locate not just within the general truth of the ministry of all, but also within the context of repeated practices of 'ordaining' people to leadership or teaching roles within the local church.

On such bases, there are Baptist traditions that have eschewed the concept of ordained ministry altogether; the Scotch Baptists, for instance, insisted on a plurality of elders in each local congregation, and were at least suspicious of any programme of education designed to fit someone for the ministry of the church. Even where a church has a single 'minister', it might be that the only distinction between the 'ordained minister' and other elders/leaders within the church is terms of employment: the minister is paid a stipend, and so enabled to work full-time in the ministry, whereas colleagues in leadership are engaged in 'tentmaking', working in secular occupations to support themselves (and their families) but giving themselves to the leadership of the church as they can. It is not too difficult to find Baptists – particularly, in my experience, ministers, who are (appropriately) wary of claiming any particular status for their office – who hold to a view like this. Such a position seems to me difficult, however. On the one hand, churches routinely employ administrators, youth leaders, worship coordinators and even cleaners, but the pastoral office is regarded by the membership as somehow different – a point which can generally be demonstrated beyond doubt by looking at agreed procedures within the congregation for the appointment of the pastor, as compared to other workers. On the other hand, such a view seems in danger of denigrating the proper Christian vocations of those who do not work full-time for the church. A leader who is fulfilling a role in child protection, or healthcare, or leadership of a mission society, or care of a family, or indeed in commerce or industry, (or indeed happens to teach theology in a Scottish university . . .) is not thereby less of a Christian minister than someone who draws a stipend from church funds.

Another view, recommended with some energy by a number of Baptist theologians in the middle years of the twentieth century, but having its origin in nineteenth-century suspicions of clericalism, sees 'ordination' as the setting apart of the pastor for certain functions. Australian Baptists, for instance, have, for forty years now, asserted that ordained ministry involves four tasks: proclamation; fellowship and nurture; teaching; and service. An older British tradition would point to the Reformed language of the 'ministry of Word and sacrament' and see preaching and liturgical presidency as crucial functions of the one ordained.

Two problems with this are readily apparent. On the one hand, it has rarely been the Baptist practice to restrict either the pulpit or the celebration of the Eucharist and the administration of baptism to the (ordained) minister. This is not insuperable, but the position requires nuance to be defensible: one might claim, for instance, that the minister is called of God and the congregation to be responsible for the pulpit ministry and liturgical celebration, and that others who serve in these capacities do so only at the minister's invitation and under his or her guidance and instruction. On the other hand, Baptist ministers have routinely moved from local church pastorate to other roles – chaplaincy in education, healthcare, the military, or elsewhere; educational roles; trans-local leadership or resourcing roles (serving as a paid officer of an association, convention or union); missionary roles; retirement; and so on. It has not commonly been Baptist practice to remove the ministerial style (i.e. the title 'Reverend') from people who so move, or to deny them the privileges accorded to serving ministers within the denomination (a personal vote at associational meetings, for example), or to re-ordain them if they should return to local church pastorate. This suggests that our implicit theology, at least, has usually assumed a continuity of ordained status even when the functions proper to that status are not being exercised, which implies an understanding of ministry that goes beyond the mere exercise of particular functions. (In fairness, it should be noted that some who have advanced this view – Arthur Dakin, long-time principal of Bristol Baptist College in England, would be a famous example – have ceased to claim the privileges and trappings of ministry when they have moved from the local church pastorate, and so have sought to live according to their confession; such integrity is of course commendable, but seems to be regarded as sufficiently eccentric by the generality of Baptists as to suggest that the theology that gives rise to it is largely foreign to the tradition).

In debates over the nature of ordination in Britain, Paul Fiddes argued for a broader 'representative' role for the ordained minister. The local church may call and invite – and indeed 'ordain' – its leaders, but their recognition remains local; the fact of ordination makes the pastor's recognition and role more than local, enabling himor her to speak within the community as a representative of the wider church, and to be recognized within the denomination as someone whose ministry and service was acknowledged and accepted beyond the local church. This was an inventive and perceptive attempt to impose some sense on the present (or rather recent; there have been significant developments since Fiddes wrote) practice within the Baptist Union of Great Britain, and has been deservedly celebrated and referenced within that context; on a wider scale, however, the proposal is perhaps less helpful. In many North American Baptist traditions, for example, the role of lay elders, although conferred solely by the local congregation, is recognized as having significance, and as conferring privilege, within the association or denomination (even within the churches of the BUGB, the role of church secretary, usually occupied by a deacon, carries with it some recognition and authority beyond the local congregation). That said, there is no doubt that an ordained minister has a status and role beyond the congregation that no other (Baptist) office can provide, and so there is certainly something of worth in Fiddes's proposal; historically and internationally, however, it probably needs to be supplemented with other accounts.

Recent Baptist theologians in Britain and America – including the present author – have proposed a 'sacramental' account of ordination, and there is good evidence to suggest that this understanding is becoming normal within the BUGB, at least in the self-understanding of ministers within that denomination.[15] There is, and has been since the rise of the Oxford movement in the first half of the nineteenth century, an instinctive Baptist, and wider evangelical, reaction against describing anything as 'sacramental'; this opposition no doubt remains stronger – for entirely appropriate reasons – in contexts where Baptists construct their identity in the face of a hostile majority Roman or Orthodox church. That said, even if opposition to the Anglican attempt to reintroduce Roman ideas of ecclesially mediated grace is appropriate, this should not blind us to important aspects of our own tradition (whether we feel comfortable using the word 'sacramental' or not). As noted above, Baptists inevitably believe in the activity of the Holy Spirit when we meet together; it is surely not impossible, therefore, to regard the act of ordination as both a recognition of the gifts the Spirit has given, and a prayer, made in confidence that it is a prayer that God will be pleased to answer, for a further bestowal and sealing of appropriate gifts on the one being set apart for ministry.

Such an account has the advantage of making sense of the distinct and permanent nature of ordination, without restricting certain ecclesial functions to the clergy. Of course, the Spirit gives gifts endlessly and variously, and is never constrained by our prayers, promises and rites; that said, when we act in conformity with the command of Scripture, we can confidently expect the Spirit to hear and answer our prayers, and to honour our actions. The setting apart of those who have been called by God through the local congregation for service through prayer and the laying on of hands is one such place (baptism and the Eucharist are others). Ordination, on this account, is a human and ecclesial act, done in accordance with the example and command of Scripture, and so done in the confidence that through, or in response to, this act, God will in turn act, and the Spirit who determines all human destinies will determine the life of this believer in ways that are consonant with a life of Christ-like sacrificial service to the churches.

Finally, a question that has troubled Baptists internationally, and in many national and local contexts, is: who is to be ordained? The question is not new in Baptist life: various justifications for the restriction of ordination to people with 'white' skin have been essayed in our history, including, within living memory, no doubt well-intentioned concerns on the part of the Conservative Baptist Foreign Mission Society that no native Congolese were educated adequately enough to take on the pastoral role.[16] The presently divisive question, however, concerns the appropriateness or otherwise of ordaining women to pastoral office. The peculiarly explosive nature of the question stems, in part, from a conviction on both sides that the issue is one of primary importance. On the one hand, a male-only ministry (a result of a belief in the rightness of male authority, or 'headship', in church, family and, perhaps, world) is held to be a clear biblical principle, presently denied by Western liberal cultures, and so a powerful test-case of whether a writer, congregation or denomination takes the Bible seriously. On the other hand, the issue is one of justice, the Spirit's gifting and God's calling: to refuse ordination to women who have clearly been called and gifted by God is a perpetuating of an inappropriate cultural sexism, and a refusal to discern and follow God's leading.

Considered in a purely historically context, this issue is complex: Thomas Edwards, in his famous *Gangraena* of 1646, was already recounting, in scandalized tones, narratives of Baptist churches in London that permitted female preachers, and there is no doubt that women were active and generally accepted in teaching ministries within the Baptist movement through much of the seventeenth century (although it should be noted that none of these women were ordained). Again, women have been active in preaching and leading among Baptists in many revival situations (the nineteenth-century St Petersburg revival was particularly notable in this respect). Further, many Baptist movements around the world have now a continuous history of ordaining women stretching back many decades; on the other hand, it is undeniably the case that the preponderant witness of Baptist history points to a male-only ministry. Even if the issue were clearer, however, history is not determinative for Baptist theology.

Baptist theology must take its final authority to be the Bible; however, there is general scholarly agreement that the biblical argument is far from clear. On the one hand, there are texts – perhaps two only (1 Cor 14.34-5 and 1 Tim 2.11-12; others, such as Eph. 5.22-33, speak of family relationships, and so cannot be applied to the life of the local church without further argument and interpretation) – that seem to forbid leadership, and particularly the teaching ministry, to women; on the other hand, it is generally accepted by New Testament scholars that there are numerous women described as fulfilling teaching ministries within the Pauline letters in particular (Junia, Phoebe and Priscilla are perhaps the most obvious, but there are several more). How to reconcile this clash of precept and example?

Beyond the Baptist world, the normal hermeneutical practice would be to privilege precept over example: theology trumps practice, and so, taking the precepts as determinative, we have to find ways of explaining away the apparently anomalous examples. Junia is assumed to be Junias, a man (despite the fact that the male name Junias is unknown in Latin sources, whereas we have hundreds of examples of women called Junia), and so on. This practice seems to me to be unBaptist, however: in defending our baptismal practice, generally regarded as our determining conviction, we have always pointed to what the apostolic churches did, not what they thought about what they did. On any natural reading of the New Testament, the apostolic churches listened to female teachers and appointed female teachers; the two isolated precepts are the anomalies, to be taken seriously as inspired Scripture, but to be understood in the light of the clear witness of the New Testament read more broadly.

Alongside this, we might consider the inevitable implications of our Baptist polity. The theological debate over the role of women in the church, where it remains live, at present endlessly revolves around questions of 'authority'; as Baptists, we know the answer to these questions. Authority belongs to Jesus; the authoritative interpretation of Jesus' call on the local church is to be determined by the gathered church; therefore, derivative authority belongs to all members of the gathered church – women as much as men and men as much as women (and children, should they be members of the church, as much as adults). A theological account of church life that suggests normative male authority in the local congregation simply cannot be accepted by Baptists, therefore: it denies our fundamental polity. Of course, it is possible to imagine an argument which extensively decoupled teaching ministry from authority, and, accepting the shared authority of all church members, nonetheless proposed a gender restriction on the ministry of teaching; I simply note that I have not encountered such a proposal, and so I see no contemporary argument being offered in defence of a male-only teaching ministry that is both theologically plausible and adequately Baptist.

The argument in the previous paragraph relies on specifically Baptist practices of Bible reading and on reflections on Baptist ecclesiology. As it happens, I am involved in pan-evangelical theological work with the UK at present, and the question of a biblical position on the role of women and men in church and family is one I have been involved in discussing in depth on several occasions. In that context, I have heard convincing and self-consciously Presbyterian or Episcopalian defences of the 'male-only ministry' position, which made sense within the hermeneutical and ecclesiological positions that define those traditions. Roman Catholic theology, with its particular account of the representative function of the priest, may call on a different set of arguments again to defend the male-only priesthood, arguments which, whether convincing or not, are distinctively Catholic. The point is that arguments over ministry and ordination must, to make any sense at all, be coordinated with the specific ecclesiology of the tradition to which they are held to apply. Baptist proponents of a male-only ministry in contemporary discussion seem always to borrow arguments from other traditions that concern questions of authority and so simply make no sense from a Baptist perspective. Until arguments that are alive to the particular nature of Baptist practice are offered, an account of specifically Baptist theology can, responsibly, give only one answer to this particular question.

Chapter 6

Christ is Lord, and the Believer is Free

The right to liberty of conscience, and the corresponding duty of toleration placed on any and every political authority, have been central components of Baptist witness since the very beginnings of the movement. No doubt there has been a measure of pragmatism in this: dissenting minorities are likely to regard toleration as an appropriate stance for governments to take. The presented defence of the position has always been theological, however, summed up sometimes in a phrase borrowed from John Knox, 'the crown rights of the Redeemer'. The standard argument relies again on what I have called the 'individualist' commitment of Baptist theology, the belief that God deals directly with each human being. Because of this, anyone who attempts to direct or control the conscience of another human being is specifically and directly interfering in a place that belongs to God alone, or, more precisely, interfering in a place that God has delegated to Christ alone, and thus usurping the 'crown rights of the Redeemer'.

Beginnings: Thomas Helwys and Roger Williams on Liberty of Conscience

Thomas Helwys's famous *Short Declaration of the Mystery of Iniquity* was written in Amsterdam in 1612, and so dates from the very earliest days of the Baptist movement.[1] The book is polemical, setting out to prove that Helwys's little band are the only true church in existence. Early in the text is a list of 'the principle matters handled in the book', which indicates that a series of condemnations of Rome, the Church of England, Puritanism, Brownism and even of John Robinson, will be offered. What is striking, however, is the fundamental ground of many, or even most, of these criticisms, the 'mystery of iniquity' of the title: men seek to occupy the place of God, claiming the right to make laws that would bind the consciences of other people, or to install priests over churches. Helwys has other points to make (he wants to defend believers' baptism and congregational government, and to repent of and condemn the practice of fleeing into exile to escape persecution, for instance), but this is the consistent thread of the work. The Roman Church is the highest evil, because the Pope has so thoroughly assumed the place of Christ that he even 'takes upon himself the power to cast soul and body to hell and to send to heaven who he will' (p. 168). When Helwys turns to the Church of England, there are passing swipes at standard Puritan targets ('your surplice, cross, churchings, burials, coops, chantings, and organs in your cathedrals', p. 172), but the main charge is again the claiming of the right to bind the human conscience: 'we come to you *Common Book*, not meddling with every particular of it, but only the most general. By what power do you make prayers and bind men to them' (p. 173). Again, the church claimed the right to enforce penitential practices, and Helwys is biting in response: 'Do you have the power also to appoint the Lord to accept these prayers and repentance? Or do you not care whether the Lord accepts them, so long as you are submitted to?' (p. 174). Even the titles pretended to by the church hierarchy are blasphemous, because they are titles that belong to Christ alone (Helwys cites several, of which perhaps the most convincing is 'Lords Spiritual', p. 176).

Helwys addresses the Puritans of his day in similar terms: their great crime, in his eyes, is their collusion with the false government of the Church of England. They see (some of) its abuses, but remain within its structures, seeking to promote reform from within. That they have some freedom to worship according to their best (Reformed) understanding within the church structures does not impress Helwys at all: '[h]e that commanded in the church the true preaching of the word, true baptism, and true administration of the Lord's Supper, the same God has also commanded true government in the church' (p. 236). Similarly he accuses them of 'giving Christ only the name of a king, but [giving] his power of government to strange lords, your lord bishops' (p. 236).

Between these two discussions, Helwys addresses directly the question of the power of the civil magistrate. The king has power to declare war, and to conscript; to employ his people and their goods in any way he might choose; to appoint governors and make laws (Helwys says 'ordinances of man', indicating perhaps the limitations he is about to discuss [p. 189]). Helwys is prepared to grant the monarch essentially unlimited powers over his earthly kingdom – but he wants to insist also on the existence of another kingdom, a heavenly kingdom, where Christ alone is king. Here, the earthly monarch has no power whatsoever: 'Christ only sits upon David's throne to order it' (p. 192). Thus, the justly famous ringing declaration:

> We still pray our lord the king that we may be free from suspicion for having any thoughts of provoking evil against those of the Romish religion in regard of their profession, if they are true and faithful subjects to the king. For we do freely profess that our lord the king has no more power over their consciences than over ours, and that is none at all. For our lord the king is but an earthly king, and he has no authority as a king but in earthly causes. If the king's people are obedient and true subjects, obeying all human laws made by the king, our lord the king can require no more. For man's religion to God is between God and themselves. The king will not answer for it. Neither may the king be judge between God and man. Let them be heretics, Turks, Jews, or whatsoever, it does not appertain to the earthly power to punish them in the least measure. (Helwys, p. 209)

The king should not pass laws that relate to matters of conscience, should not appoint church officers, should not judge or rule in matters of religion and should not allow patterns of worship to be imposed on his people.

Helwys's point is simple: Christ is king over every human conscience, and Christ has chosen to woo, not to compel. If another seeks to govern the human conscience in a way specifically rejected by its one true king, whoever that other may be, he is, simply and precisely, setting himself up as Antichrist.

One surviving copy of Helwys's work contains a handwritten dedication directly to King James:

> Hear, O King, and despise not the counsel of the poor, and let their complaints come before thee. The king is a mortal man and not God, therefore has no power over the immortal souls of his subjects, to make laws and ordinances for them, and to set spiritual lords over them. If the king has authority to make spiritual lords and laws, then he is an immortal God and not a mortal man. O King, be not seduced by deceivers to sin against God whom you ought to obey, nor against your poor subjects who ought and will obey you in all things with body, life, and goods, or else let their lives be taken from the earth. God save the king.[2]

King James is (in danger of) putting himself in the place of God. Toleration must be extended, on profoundly theological grounds.

Helwys concerns himself directly with the interference of the monarch in religious affairs, no doubt because that was the reality in his day: in England, at least (James's role in the Scots Kirk was less clear), the monarch was – and is – styled supreme governor of the Church of England, and so the question of the usurpation of the 'crown rights of the Redeemer' was most properly addressed directly to the monarch. The logic of Helwys's position, however, and his denunciations of the papacy, indicate that modern notions of 'the separation of church and state' are, while perhaps a necessary consequence of his position, certainly not the heart of it. Any interference, by anybody, in the freedom of the believer to follow his or her conscience in matters of religious practice is theologically inappropriate and indeed a trespassing on ground that belongs to Christ alone.

The Anglican Bishops of his day were to be condemned, not because they were state appointments, but because they imposed patterns of worship and devotion on their people – they were, in Helwys's previously quoted words, 'strange lords' who were attempting to stand in the place of Christ.

Just as the founder of the first Baptist church in England was committed to liberty of conscience, so too was the case in America. Roger Williams's commitment to Baptist principles was brief, but he has the honour of being the organizer of the first Baptist congregation on American soil, when he led some, at least, of his Providence congregation into accepting baptism and forming a new church there. A few months later he left the church, questioning (as Smyth had done) the propriety of baptism by one not himself baptized (Williams had been baptized by one Ezekiel Holliman, who he then immediately baptized in turn); in his later life, he adopted the position that the true church had died, and so that a Christian life was not possible unless and until God raised up a new apostle to re-found the church. His commitment to religious liberty was much more lasting than his Baptist principles, perhaps resulting from first-hand observation of persecution during his youth in London. Although he accepted Anglican ordination following his graduation from Cambridge in 1627, he was a convinced Separatist by 1629, and soon chose to depart for the American colonies. The extent of his commitment to Separatist ecclesiology may be judged by his refusal of the attractive pulpit at Boston on the grounds that he regarded the church as too closely entangled with the governing authorities. In 1635 he was tried and convicted for holding various beliefs, including that it was improper to attend parish worship in England, and that the civil magistrate 'power extends only to the Bodies and Goods, and outward State of men'.

The first of these charges shows that Williams was as convinced of the apostasy of the Church of England as Helwys had been; the second relates to his particular construction of liberty of conscience. As was common, he divided the Ten Commandments into two 'tables', covering duty to God and duty to neighbour. The magistrate, on Williams's telling, could police the second table, but never the first. Idolatry and blasphemy were matters that God would judge, and no human being should seek to stand in God's place. The court intended to return him to England, where his fate would no doubt have been unpleasant; he escaped and spent some months with Native Americans that he had befriended, learning their language in the missionary cause. Then, with several others, he founded Providence, a small farmstead outside the jurisdiction of Massachusetts Bay. In the mid-1640s, Williams was in London, seeking a charter to make Providence a recognized colony (the charter for Rhode Island was finally granted in 1663, famously enshrining religious freedom); there he wrote his *Bloudy Tenent of Persecution* (1644), a general appeal to Parliament during the Civil War for religious liberty.[3]

Williams makes use of some earlier separatist pamphlets, none of them pre-dating Helwys, however.[4] Williams's particular object is what he calls is 'persecution for the cause of conscience': this, he suggests, might take three forms: sanction imposed for beliefs; sanction imposed for worshipping in particular modes; or sanction imposed for refusing to be constrained to worship in unacceptable ways. The book was written quickly, and is rather disorganized, but Williams's points are clear and his prose powerful. He argues that persecution is ineffective – but this is a theological point, not a pragmatic one: 'the Country takes the Alarum to expell that fog or mist of Errour, Heresie, Blasphemy (as is supposed) with Swords and Guns; whereas tis Light alone, even Light from the bright shining Sunne of Righteousnesse, which is able, in the soules and consciences of men to dispell and scatter such fogges and darknesse' (Williams, p. 30). Christ alone is able to command the human conscience; the magistrate who tries is as foolish and arrogant as King Canute was in his attempt to command the tides.

Williams bases his arguments extensively on biblical exegesis, but there are also some crucial underlying conceptual distinctions. One in particular is important for understanding the concept of religious liberty more generally, the distinction between 'morality' and 'religion'.[5] The notion that the state should not enforce or prohibit practices of belief or devotion is relatively easy to understand, but in modern multicultural contexts we have grown used to the fact that it is in areas of religious ethics that the debate becomes murky: should a Jewish shop worker be permitted to demand alterations to his or her working conditions to prevent him or her from coming into contact with pork products? Can a health worker who is opposed on religious grounds to the practice of abortion seek exemption from certain duties? Should religious practices (e.g. the wearing of ritual headgear, or practices of ritual slaughter of animals for consumption) be permitted even when they breach laws, rules or guidelines (perhaps concerning health and safety, or animal welfare) that apply generally to society?

Williams's distinction is an attempt to navigate through such questions.

Religion, for Williams, is fundamentally a matter of the orientation of the heart towards God and the gospel. Morality concerns only conformity in outward actions. There is, of course, overlap: a right orientation of the heart will tend to produce certain sorts of outward actions, so religion can and does promote morality. For morality as much as for worship, however, an act is only adequately religious if it is performed out of a right orientation of the heart, and this is what government cannot legislate for. The true Christian will refrain from stealing because of a commitment to following Christ and a fear of God, not because of a fear of the local law enforcement agencies; the government may legislate against stealing, as an outward act, but has no business in trying to discern the motivation behind someone's compliance with the legislated morality and no ability to coerce people to act out of a preferred motivation.

This does not yet quite rule out state coercion of religious practice: as Archbishop Parker would later point out in defending the oppressive and shameful Anglican settlement of 1662, even the Clarendon Code demanded only outward conformity, and did not attempt to police convictions and beliefs. Williams's response would be similar to that John Owen made to Parker: that in specifically religious matters – anything involving naming or invoking God – the distinction between outward act and inner orientation cannot be sustained, or not without forcing people into the sins of hypocrisy and blasphemy. The magistrate can force me not to steal, but cannot force me to love God or feel sorrow for my sin; and to force me to say that I love God, or to recite a prayer of repentance, is to force me into hypocrisy, which is unacceptable. For Williams, the particular issue was the swearing of an oath of loyalty, required of all settlers in the Bay colony. In traditional style, the oath began with a formula of swearing by 'the great and dreadful Name of the Ever-living God' and ended with a plea for divine aid: 'So help me God in the Lord Jesus Christ'. Williams was convinced that the one who was not a true believer could not in good conscience make the prayer at the end; he also believed that the true believer could not, in good conscience, swear in God's name, because churches, not civil states, should be established by vows to God. No-one, therefore, should be compelled to take this oath, which was nevertheless at the heart of the civil settlement of Massachusetts Bay.

Williams therefore had an uncompromising view of the nature of liberty of conscience, but actually a very restricted view of its scope. In each of the modern examples I gave in passing above, this would lead Williams to be unsympathetic to the claims for exemptions or special treatment on grounds of conscience. In part this is because his experience of religious traditions was limited to forms of Protestant Christianity that had few, if any, commitments to ritual practice or dress, and so he could not have imagined that abstinence from certain foods, or the wearing of certain garments, could be a matter of conscience as central to a religious orientation as the making of oaths and the offering of prayers. In part, also, Williams lived in a fairly monocultural world and was able to assume with little argument that there was a 'natural law' written on the hearts of all people that told them what was right and wrong in most situations. So later, when the question of exemption from service in the militia on grounds of conscientious objection arose in Providence, Williams was dismissive: this was a civil matter, and the civil government had the right to demand and, if need be, to compel obedience.[6] Arguably, Williams's conception of what properly belonged to the sphere of religion was too narrow (and, concomitantly, his understanding of the level of moral intuition common to all humanity far too wide); however, his grasp of the theological and pragmatic inviolability of that sphere was secure and profound.

Isaac Backus and Later Discussions of Liberty of Conscience

It would not be difficult to highlight many later Baptist defenders of the principle of liberty of conscience. Perhaps the greatest was Isaac Backus, who rescued Williams's name from obscurity in his famous historical work. Backus extended the reach of belief in liberty of conscience into areas Williams would have regarded as part of the civil settlement, notably including taxation. The great campaign for which Backus is remembered is the resistance to compulsory church taxes, which were common across New England as the means for supporting the ministers of the majority, Congregational, churches. (As the eighteenth century progressed, there were laws passed the allowed dissenters – generally Baptists, Quakers and Anglicans – to not pay the taxes, but the laws were patchy, not always honoured, and to register as a dissenter was bureaucratically complex and financially costly.)

Backus agreed with Williams that God had instituted government, but he suggested that there were in fact two spheres of government instituted by God: civil and ecclesiastical, with separate spheres of responsibility.[7] The civil government is to encompass all people, the righteous and the wicked, and to restrain evil by forceful compulsion of outward acts; the ecclesiastical government is to serve the righteous only and separate itself from all visible sin; it is not to use compulsion. Because of this difference, it is impossible for a single government to serve adequately in both spheres. Backus believed that historically, whenever a government tried to combine the two functions it ended up using coercion in an attempt to control the consciences of the people. This is wrong on many levels:

> The business of laws is not to provide for the truth of opinions, but for the safety and security of the commonwealth, and of every man's goods and person; and so it ought to be; for truth certainly would do well enough if she were once left to shift for herself. She seldom has received, and I fear never will receive, much assistance from the power of great men; to whom she is but rarely known, and more rarely welcome. She is not taught by laws, nor has she any need of force to procure her entrance into the minds of men. Errors indeed prevail by the existence of foreign and borrowed succours.[8]

Backus intertwines three senses of liberty. First, it is the condition in which we are able to do as our reason dictates; second, it is the salvific experience of being set free from sin and guilt, and being able to approach the throne of grace; third, it is the legal permission to dispose of one's own goods and person as one chooses. Importantly, in talking about liberty of conscience Backus is not merely referring to the third sense here, but to a combination of all three. Further, he does not see conscience as immediate or untutored; liberty of conscience implies a solemn and sacred duty of searching out the will of God from the Scriptures, and a solemn and sacred right of following what one finds there without interference or imposition.

The settlement of pastors over a people is a paradigmatic case: 'if we may not settle and support a minister agreeable to our own consciences, where is liberty of conscience?' This immediately means that a general taxation for the support of a particular pastoral ministry must be inappropriate: 'by what law, or with what equity, are we forced to pay for the settlement of another with whom we cannot in conscience join!'[9] That said, Backus does not believe that his position is noticeably different from that of Williams; this is merely an argument from their shared position that Williams happened to not see.

In fact, Backus could be argued to be narrower in his conception than Williams, in that his major criticism of Williams concerns the extent to which religious duties are knowable by natural revelation. No doubt reflecting his eighteenth-century context, Backus is much more hopeful about the ability of reason to discern the duties proper to humanity in the religious sphere; and suggests that those duties knowable by reason may properly be legislated for. Thus, Backus would be prepared to allow legislation for a practice of prayer, which Williams never would have. However, it is important to note that this difference, like the one over taxation, is not a difference of principle, but a difference of understanding in how that principle applies to particular circumstances. For another example of this point, consider the somewhat regular claim that Backus wanted to exclude Roman Catholics from the legislature of Massachusetts; the lines generally quoted in defence of this claim are in fact misquoted, as they indicate sentiments Backus puts into the mouths of his opponents in the course of discussing his argument. That said, he has genuine hesitations, based in part on a belief that Roman Catholic believers have taken an oath of unquestioning obedience to a foreign territorial ruler, the Pope, and as such are dangerous people to have in the legislature.

This is a fairly regular argument in the history of debates over liberty of conscience in Britain – Backus' employment of it in the American context is more eccentric – forming a major plank of opposition to the Catholic Relief Act of 1829 (and giving the reason for the strong restrictions still placed on the Jesuits and other orders under the Act, and for the specific clauses of the oath required of any Catholic member of parliament). The extent to which it is a true representation of the claims of the Pope at any point in history after the defeat of the Spanish Armada might reasonably be questioned, but that is not particularly the point here. The cautions of Backus – and those of many others – concerning the presence of Catholic members of legislative bodies are not based on any restriction of liberty of conscience, but upon a civil belief that those who are demonstrably not loyal to the commonwealth, in purely political terms, should not be permitted to take a part in the governing of the commonwealth.

Baptist accounts of liberty of conscience, then, have a fairly fixed theological basis from Helwys down to Backus and indeed beyond, into the middle of the nineteenth century. What changes is the way this theological commitment is applied, on the basis of other understandings. Helwys and Williams lived in an age that assumed totalitarian government; in this context their understanding of the extent of the application of an appeal to liberty of conscience was necessarily limited. Living today in the context of liberal democracy (as an ideal, if sometimes imperfectly realized), the scope of liberty of conscience is much broader. To take one of my earlier examples, legislation that requires the wearing of protective headgear, one of the general principles of liberal democracy is that I have a right to endanger myself, but not others (I am not here arguing for the rightness or wrongness of this principle, merely stating its existence). This would suggest that health and safety laws concerned with personal protection can and should be set aside fairly readily if there is a convincing reason: the state's ability to interfere in practices concerning personal safety is rather weak. If, for whatever reason, the safety of others was imperilled, in a liberal democracy the claim that liberty of conscience applied in this area would be felt to be less strong, because it is a claim which recognizes, without defining, that there is a sphere proper to civic government in which appeals to 'conscience' carry no force.

Liberty of Conscience and Believers' Baptism

There is another twist in the tale to be told, with E. Y. Mullins's recasting of liberty of conscience in the influential language of 'soul competency' in the early part of the twentieth century. Before any treatment of that, however, I turn away from the history to my construction of Baptist theology. In the previous chapter I identified what I there called an 'individualistic' strand in Baptist theology, a controlling belief that God in Christ deals directly with each person. There, I drew out the practice of believers' baptism as a natural concomitant of this belief (along with a commitment to congregational church government); the point now, obvious as soon as stated, is that this commitment to the direct and personal nature of God's dealings with women and men sits very naturally with a commitment to liberty of conscience also.

This point can be further developed both positively and negatively. Positively, the Baptist commitment to liberty of conscience, as expounded in my readings of Helwys, Williams and Backus above, makes no sense without a belief that the individual human being, of whatever level of education, social status, gender or ethnicity, is by God's grace, a recipient of God's direct address and is directly responsible to God for her or his actions. As Helwys had it, speaking of the people's religious belief and practice, 'the king will not answer for it'. Neither, we may add, will any bishop, priest or minister, or indeed any spouse, parent or godparent. This is not to deny a proper duty placed upon family members, ordained ministers – and indeed, in Baptist understanding, all church members – to witness wherever possible to the truth as they best know it, to seek to bring up a child, specifically, in the life and doctrine of the church, and to commend to him or her the offers and claims of Christ. All of this, however, is a personal religious duty, not a responsibility for the life or soul of another. Christ will woo the sinner's heart directly, using sometimes the services of others as means or occasion, of course, but still, the sinner's relationship to God is a matter for which he or she shall answer and no other.

This is, to make the point again, a remarkable affirmation of the dignity God grants by grace to all human beings. Roger Williams was involved in the case of Joshua Verdin, who was exiled from Providence, not because he refused to attend public worship there, but because he sought to prevent his wife from attending, beating her harshly in attempting to impose what he understood to be his proper authority over her. This authority – the husband's right, and indeed duty, to impose his religious convictions upon his wife (and children and servants) – would have been recognized in the seventeenth century by all civil and religious authorities, except those in Providence (and, it should be added, by other similar religious radicals). She was no chattel, but a person in her own right, called by God to the awesome responsibility of making her own decision about the call of Christ on her life. As a result, she had both right and duty to disobey her husband in the following of her own conscience. One writer has claimed in regard of this case that 'Providence was the first civil government to recognize these feminine rights as a natural and civil right'.[10] This claim may be slightly ambitious, but certainly the case indicates that a conviction concerning liberty of conscience does establish personal dignity in far-reaching and countercultural ways.

To develop the original point negatively, if it is indeed the case that Christ speaks directly to the human soul, then the government has no right or competence to intervene in that relationship. On a theological account, after all, the magistrate's authority is purely derivative, given by God for the maintenance of relative peace and good order in the earthly city during the years of God's patience before the return of Christ. The magistrate who claims authority beyond that which God has permitted is overstepping the bounds established by God and has no legitimacy, at least for the offending decisions or actions. In both Britain and America, of course, this notion of governments over-reaching their authority was alive and powerful in the culture of the seventeenth and (in America) the eighteenth centuries. In a marvellous rhetorical linkage, Isaac Backus points out that the charge levied on Baptists for obtaining certificates of exemption from their taxes in New England happened to be equal to the tea-tax that had sparked the revolution. His point could not be clearer: government imposition of religion is as pernicious as government imposition of duties on an unrepresented people. The great cry of freedom, if it is to mean anything, must challenge the latter as vigorously as the former.

Today, the practice of believers' baptism still acts as a powerful witness for religious liberty. The child who has grown up within the church fellowship and who seeks baptism no doubt brings joy to his or her parents; but the child also witnesses that they had no right and no ability under God to determine its religious identity; the convert from without the community who seeks baptism – particularly if baptized, or otherwise received into a religious community, as an infant – is acknowledging that Christ alone is Lord of their conscience, and so that previous attempts by others to determine their life and beliefs were ineffective and improper. The point holds, of course, not just for those coming to Baptist convictions, but for all human beings: they must be allowed to follow their consciences into whatever form of religious practice seems best to them. This is presently a live issue in parts of Eastern Europe, in particular, where (following the collapse of Communism) a significant measure of religious nationalism has grown up in certain states, generally assuming, often stating and sometimes enacting legally the idea that to be a 'true' citizen of the nation is to belong to the ancient religion (often the Roman Catholic Church, or a local Orthodox Church, but sometimes also Islam). In such a context, informal discrimination and legal persecution are ongoing realities, and Baptists are working actively to secure freedom of conscience not just for themselves, but for others.[11]

E. Y. Mullins and 'Soul Competency'

I have already given some space to Edgar Y. Mullins and his influence in his long tenure as president of the Southern Seminary in Louisville, Kentucky. In 1908, Mullins published a book entitled *The Axioms of Religion: A New Interpretation of the Baptist Faith*.[12] The aim of the book was, as the subtitle indicates, to offer a re-narration of Baptist theology which would be convincing to the wider church and world. Mullins narrates the history of religion since the Reformation as fundamentally a conflict between a belief in the direct access of the soul to God, and a belief that the soul's access to God is only indirect (p. 109). He identifies the genius of Protestantism with the former and the core of Roman Catholicism with the latter, and then proceeds to evaluate different Protestant traditions on this basis, showing that the Baptist tradition is most purely and properly true to this principle throughout its faith and polity.

More basically, Mullins offers an account of six axioms to which, he claims, all Baptists hold, and which will adequately explain the Baptist position to outsiders. These are as follows:

1. The theological axiom: the holy and loving God has a right to be sovereign
2. The religious axiom: all souls have an equal right to direct access to God
3. The ecclesiastical axiom: all believers have a right to equal privileges in the church
4. The moral axiom: to be responsible, man must be free
5. The religio-civic axiom: a free church in a free state
6. The social axiom: love your neighbour as yourself (Mullins, pp. 73–4).

Underlying all of these, Mullins suggested, was the core notion of 'soul competency', which he regarded (p. 53) and defended (pp. 59–69) as the unique contribution of the Baptists to history. He defined soul competency carefully, first insisting that it is not an assertion of human autonomy: '[o]f course, this means a competency under God, not a competency in the sense of human self-sufficiency' (p. 53). After this insistence, he discusses the importance of this doctrine in terms of both what it denies and what it affirms. It denies any account of mediation in spiritual matters or, as Mullins puts it, 'episcopacy and infant baptism, and every form of religion by proxy' (p. 54). It affirms, variously: the separation of church and state, justification by faith alone, regeneration, and the gathered church of professed believers (pp. 54–5). Mullins cheerfully makes the link between soul competency and democracy, in church life (p. 55) and in national life ('[w]e are approaching the Baptist age of the world, because we are approaching the age of the triumph of democracy'; this after the most astonishing typological reading of the shapes of the Federal flag, p. 275).

'Soul competency' is not language one can imagine Helwys, Williams or Backus using, and not language that – to the best of my knowledge – is found in any pre-1900 mainstream Baptist statement. That does not make it wrong, of course, but it does invite us to ask about the extent to which the idea is a development of themes already innate in the tradition and the extent to which it is a new departure (and whether, as such, it is justified or not). The early responses to the idea were cautiously positive, tending to accept that it was an acceptable reformulation of one strand of Baptist thought, but that it ignored the second necessary pole, the focus on the local congregation.[13] In its narrow statement, this is certainly fair criticism, but Mullins cannot be generally regarded as neglecting the congregational principle, and so perhaps a better statement of the concern would be that in reducing his six axioms to this one point, Mullins does not make it clear how his obvious commitment to congregational government relates to his idea of soul competency.

An alternative defence might focus on Mullins's particular claims for soul competency: it is not the centre of things – that has to be Christ) or the basic arbiter of truth – Scripture, of course – rather, it is that single distinctive that sets the Baptists apart from all other groups. Much as John Wesley saw in the doctrine of Christian perfection the truth that, while not most important in the faith, had been uniquely entrusted to the Methodists, so Mullins seems to believe that the particular, and vital, gift of the Baptists to the broader (Protestant) church is the doctrine of soul competency. Better, of course, to lose this than salvation by faith alone, or scriptural authority, or the deity of Christ; but it remains true, and the particular communal charism of Baptist Christians is to witness to its truth and its proper importance. All that said, Mullins's language became so generally accepted that it formed the natural mode of expression of a Baptist World Alliance declaration of 1939, which asserts that '[w]orthy religion rests on the conviction that the individual soul is competent to deal directly with God, and has the right and the need of this direct dealing'.[14]

I have been essaying what I have called an intense individualism in Baptist theology in this book; how does that relate to soul competency? I note, first, that Mullins's idea was criticized precisely for its alleged individualism by a later president of the Baptist World Alliance.[15] On the basis of my comments above, however, I am not sure that this criticism stands; Baptist theology can never be reduced to a belief that every particular person is a separated spiritual entity, needing no church life, no Christian fellowship, to survive – but Mullins never imagined such a thing. Baptist theology will, however, as I have already insisted, demand that the call of Christ to each particular person – to each individual, if the word is allowed to refer without the suspicious taints it carries in some recent academic work – is direct and inviolable. I take it that it is this reality to which Mullins in gesturing in his language of 'soul competency', and, as such, I find his intention wholly laudable.

That said, the term chosen, 'soul competency', and the explanation given of it, seem to invite an unhappy misunderstanding, particularly in the cultural context in which Mullins wrote. As I suggested in the previous chapter, the Baptist vision can easily be mistaken for an importation of democracy into church life, and Mullins not only does nothing to resist that, but positively encourages it. He seems to align Baptist church polity with American democracy as the highest vision of human community. This is unacceptable. If Baptists are faithful to their original Scriptural vision, they will insist that such an elevation of American democracy is simple idolatry, just as any similar elevation of any other earthly polity would be. Baptist life was forged in the fires of Anglicans, Presbyterians, Congregationalists and Catholics, each trying to identify one or another political settlement with the Kingdom of God; in missionary work in Continental Europe and Central Asia we discovered Lutherans, Reformed and the Orthodox trying to do the same thing. We named each one as Antichrist, because Christ's Kingdom must never be conflated with any of the kingdoms of this world. Any attempted spiritual elevation of American polity into the Kingdom of Christ must be met by Baptists with the same uncompromising rejection that we offered to all those others. Mullins's vision, as developed by him, to some extent, and certainly by those after him, is dangerously syncretistic. American democracy is not an anticipation of the Kingdom of God any more than the British Puritan Commonwealth or the Massachusetts Congregational settlement were; and it, like them, must never be treated as such. Mullins was unclear on this point and so departed in a profound way from the Baptist vision of Helwys, Williams and Backus.

There is a further problem with the term 'soul competency', one which Mullins sought to guard against, but perhaps unwittingly invited. The term seems to imply that every particular person has an innate ability to find access to the divine. East of Eden, however, access to God is never innate but always by gracious gift. Rather than asserting universal competency in approaching the divine and castigating other Christian traditions for imposing needless intermediaries, we should assert universal human incompetence and castigate other Christian traditions for pretending that their various proposed intermediaries might alleviate the problem in any way at all. Helwys's complaint about Anglican practices of penitence was not that they interfered with the naturally available direct access of the penitent to God, but that they consisted of human ceremonies which were presumed to bind God down to acting in particular ways. The traditional Baptist witness is that all souls are utterly incompetent when it comes to divine things, and the intervention of priests, bishops and popes does not change that. Mullins's reversal of the traditional language was a brilliant apologetic move in the context of his culture, but, precisely because of this, it is in grave danger of being profoundly misleading on a central point of doctrine. Christ is Lord, not the believer. Christ alone sovereignly makes himself available. The believer has no competence, only the divinely granted freedom to pursue and obey Christ's call.

Liberty of Conscience Today

As already noted, liberty of conscience remains a live issue for Baptists across the world and – at their best – Baptists have stood for liberty of conscience for all, not just for themselves. Perhaps the most important question here is a disputed one in the tradition: can liberty of conscience be mitigated if there is a threat to the stability of the commonwealth? Helwys thought it could; Williams, on the other hand, thought that it could not. To put the question in concrete terms, imagine the existence of a congregation of religious believers – they may be Muslim, but they may equally be Hindu, Buddhist, Christian, or indeed specifically Baptist – whose practices of worship actively promote civil disobedience, or even the violent overthrow of the political order under which they exist. Does their active threat to the state mean that their liberty of conscience must be set aside, or does liberty of conscience trump even security requirements?

This is an important question; there is an oft-stated political doctrine around today that the security of the populace is the over-riding duty of government. Under a classic account of modern liberal democracy this is true, but it is also qualified: such a duty does not permit the abrogation of certain basic moral limits on state action. A recent Baptist World Alliance statement makes the point very well, discussing torture.[16] It begins with an assertion of the political point: '[g]overnments are responsible for protecting their people', and locates this responsibility in Scripture with an appeal to Rom. 13. It goes on, however, to insist that 'governments are not permitted to act in absolutely any way that might seem effective to protect national security. Protecting citizens from harm is a very high good, but it is not such an absolute good that it can be defended "by any means necessary"'. Torture is identified as one of three acts that, according to international law, can never be justified (the others being slavery and genocide). On this witness (and this witness, although specifically Baptist, accords with the standards of every body that can credibly claim to represent the international community at present), a state should allow the continuation of a real and present threat to national security rather than to resort to torture. This is a straightforward moral requirement that cannot be circumvented.

On a Baptist understanding, the protection of liberty of conscience stands also as a basic moral requirement that cannot be circumvented. That said, there is a legitimate and pressing debate to be had on the point at which the legitimate limits of liberty of conscience are reached. I take it that most or all Baptists would believe that the use of indiscriminate violence (e.g. the planting of a terrorist bomb) would transgress these limits; what of preaching that encouraged others to use indiscriminate violence? If that is also unacceptable, what of preaching that so emphasized the horror and evil of a particular cultural situation that the use of indiscriminate violence was, although never recommended, potentially legitimated in the minds of the hearers? What, in all of this, of the practice or promotion of non-violent civil disobedience? I am not sure that Baptist theology has adequately faced these questions, and yet they seem pressing in many states around the world today.

Perhaps the most able interpreter of the classical Baptist tradition on this point today is Nigel Wright, principal of Spurgeon's College in London, and former president of the Baptist Union of Great Britain.[17] Wright reinterprets classical Baptist commitments on the basis of a reading on the one hand, of sixteenth-century Anabaptist sources, and on the other hand, of post-modern political theory. Politically, the state, like any other powerful organization, is always to be suspected, and almost always to be feared and resisted; its plausible legitimations are in fact concealed attempts to impose a hegemonic power structure on the people. Theologically, the state is a part of the fallen-but-being-redeemed created order, and so always this side of the Eschaton, something to be questioned and mistrusted. On this basis, the calling of the church is to maintain what Wright calls 'a critical distance' from the state; 'Christians . . . will not surrender the government of the church to any power other than Christ'.[18]

That said, Wright is alive to the problems inherent in the concept of toleration that I have just outlined. Equally, he is convinced of the necessity of such a concept of toleration. As he puts it:

> For free church Christians tolerance has a theological basis rooted both in the illogicality of intolerance and the nature of Christian belief. Religious intolerance proceeds from the belief that those who are in error are dangerous to the common good and so should be rooted out. But the measures taken against them prove to be more dangerous to the common good than their errors themselves . . . If true faith is God-given and sincere then it cannot by its nature be instilled by coercive or persecutory methods.[19]

The echoes of Helwys and Williams are inescapable: persecution is pragmatically foolish, since it can never convince the heart. Here, however, the vision of liberty of conscience is spelt out in terms conducive to the politics of the twenty-first century, just as Helwys and Williams spelt it out in seventeenth-century terms, Backus in eighteenth-century terms and Mullins in twentieth-century terms.

For all, the immediate Lordship of Christ over the individual human soul is central; how this is worked out in practice for each depends on other commitments, concerning the nature of government, the truth available to human beings in nature and so on. There have been and will be arguments by Baptists over these secondary, yet decisive, questions; however, the core commitment to liberty of conscience stands as a constant witness through our history.

Chapter 7

Making Disciples: Mission and Holiness

'Go therefore and make disciples of all nations, baptizing them in the name of the Father and of the Son and of the Holy Spirit, and teaching them to obey everything that I have commanded you' (Mt 28.19-20, NRSV). In these words of Jesus two further central Baptist concerns are linked: mission and holiness. On the one hand, the missionary spirit within Baptist life has (almost) always been strong, a commitment to see new converts brought into the church; on the other hand, a commitment to the visible holiness of the church demands a process of moral formation after conversion, so that church members are enabled to live up to the high calling that their status confers. These two themes will be addressed in this chapter.

'Every Baptist a Missionary'

From Helwys's insistence that his people must return to England, even in the face of persecution, because of a duty to evangelize their home nation and Roger Williams's learning of native tongues in order to win converts, through Fuller, Carey and the beginnings of the modern missionary movement, to leading contemporary missiologists such as David Bosch or Orlando Costas, it is not difficult to find Baptists whose contributions to the theory and practice of Christian mission are significant. Perhaps the most astonishing example of the Baptist commitment to mission, however, is the remarkable figure of Johann Gerhard Oncken, whose vision and missionary efforts shaped Baptist life across Continental Europe.

Oncken has been described as 'a one-man mission society, theological seminary, and literature distribution center'.[1] From nothing, the Union of Associated Churches of Baptized Christians grew to 165 churches with over 30,000 members in his lifetime; it had established a seminary and had congregations in a dozen or more European nations. He founded a publishing house and personally distributed over two million Bibles, along with countless tracts. (In a letter appealing for funds, published in 1857 in the *Gospel Herald*, Oncken claimed that up to that point over eight million tracts had been distributed.) Many of the churches were planted by Oncken himself, who was tireless in his missionary efforts; he was also, however, committed to raising up younger leaders, who were trained to be as aggressively evangelistic as he himself was. He ruled the Union almost autocratically by the sheer force of his reputation and personality. His famous motto was '*Jeder Baptist ein Missionar*' ('every Baptist a missionary'); more than this, his ecclesiology emphasized that the primary role of the local church, and the only rationale for associations, was missional. Oncken did not have a missiology as a part of his theology; he had a theology that was shaped by mission from beginning to end.

In Oncken's vision, of course, there is a background of German pietism, overlaid with evangelical experience gained as a young man in the United Kingdom, and a classically Baptist individualism: personal conversion, personal commitment to Christ and personal experience of the work of the Spirit are central themes. To these, Oncken added a personal commitment to evangelism. Not to be actively involved in mission work was, in his view, sufficient to disqualify one from church membership (he insisted not only that every church member have an answer to the question 'what are you going to do to serve Christ?' but that the answer be recorded in writing so that the member could be held accountable for his or her response). Congregations of missionary disciples should be equally missionary, as the Union 'Protokol' had it: '[e]very apostolic Christian church must be a Mission Society'.[2]

As noted above, Oncken is only one example. The missionary impulse runs deep in Baptist identity. It is not, of course, a uniquely Baptist theme, but there is perhaps a distinctively Baptist emphasis on the theme; it is difficult to think of another Christian tradition that has so uniformly seen mission as being so central to its vision of the life of the church. (As should have been clear from the discussion in Chapter 2 above, the 'anti-missions movement' which gave rise to the Primitive Baptists was not, despite its name, opposed to the work of mission; rather, it was opposed to the idea that mission should be the work of organizations separated from the local church. The Primitive impulse was negative – an opposition to Christian organizations that were regarded as unhelpful and unbiblical – rather than positive, but it could actually be read, generously perhaps, as an expression of this Baptist emphasis on mission: this work is not something that can safely be surrendered by the local church, because it is so central to what it is to be the church, in a Baptist understanding.)

In keeping with the theme of the book, my intention here is to give an account, first of the theological emphases that led to the centrality of mission for Baptists, and then of some theological themes that have been shaped by the relentless focus on mission. I do not therefore intend to describe missions history in any detail here, except insofar as it supplies useful illustrations of theological themes. Baptist missions have not been exempt from the strengths or the weaknesses of the contemporary Protestant missions movement, being, for example, sometimes far too willing to become an arm of the colonizing state, and sometimes a courageous voice of protest against colonial exploitation. Theology is, at least in part, about the generation of a vision of what the church should be under Christ; if, historically, that vision is never actually achieved, it is nonetheless a useful exercise to picture clearly the goal being aimed at.

Mission and Individualism: The Place of the Child in Baptist Life

If Baptists are more relentlessly focused on mission than other Christian traditions, it is appropriate to ask if there is anything in Baptist theology which might be seen as causing that focus. One obvious candidate is the refusal to baptize children of church members: because of this, a Baptist church is always very visibly one generation away from extinction: in other traditions, children are incorporated into the church at birth (or soon afterwards);

while (particularly in the modern West) there might be a genuine issue of retaining children as they grow, they have been incorporated into the church in baptism. For Baptists, baptism and church membership is something the child must request for him or herself when it is ready to confess his or her own faith in Christ. Baptist work with children could therefore be regarded as missional rather than catechetical: it is a reaching out to those not yet in the church rather than a nurture of those who are.

This is a deduction from baptismal practice and one which has met some resistance within Baptist life, particularly, perhaps, since the nineteenth-century Western romanticization of childhood. An interesting alternative point of view is maintained in the Constitution of the Baptist Union of Victoria (Australia). The BUV has a doctrinal basis, which is essentially a brief summary of basic Christian doctrine, its only distinctively Baptist element being the definition of baptism; this is supplemented by a longer statement of 'Principles and Ideals of the Baptist Faith' in which Baptist distinctives are spelt out. The first of these is a discussion of 'the child in the kingdom', which claims:

> Baptists believe that infants are God's little ones, whether children of Christian or non-Christian parents, and accept without modification the word of the Lord, 'Of such is the Kingdom of Heaven'. This Christian view of the child makes the external act of 'Infant Baptism' unnecessary.

The statement goes on to introduce the notion of a 'stage of personal responsibility' in which personal sin is a possibility, and the gospel can be proposed for belief. This might read as simple Pelagianism, except that the doctrinal basis insists on '[t]he fallen, sinful, and lost estate of all mankind'; presumably the belief implied is that, before the commission of personal sin, Christ's atoning work is adequate to save the fallen human infant without any requirement of faith. Children are not able to be church members, however: that privilege is clearly restricted to those who have come to a personal faith.

It is fair to say that this defence of the practice of believers' baptism on the basis of there being no need for an infant to be baptized is unusual within Baptist history, although other examples can certainly be found. More normally, the defence turns on the fact that the proper practice of baptism requires that it be restricted to those candidates who can give an account of their faith and who express their own desire to be baptized. The age at which a child might be competent to do this is, of course, an open question: in Britain, baptisms of pre-teen children are extremely rare; in North American traditions, by contrast, eight is often identified as the age at which requests for baptism might generally be taken seriously; it is even possible to find Baptist churches that will offer baptism to pre-school children.

In Baptist practice, a service of infant dedication or presentation was fairly widely adopted around the world in the twentieth century; in this service, the child is presented before the church, promises are made by parents (and sometimes congregation) concerning the upbringing of the child in the Christian faith, and prayers of blessing are pronounced over the child. Noting that the catechumenate was originally a period of instruction preceding baptism, it is possible to see the combination of the act of dedication and the provision of children's instruction by the local church as an enrolling of the child in the catechumenate; she or he becomes one who is undergoing instruction and preparing for the moment when she or he will request baptism.

Such an understanding does not, however, change the fact that work with children in a Baptist context is explicitly missional; rather it recognizes that there are appropriately varying missional practices for different people in different contexts. Roger Williams's suggestion that a child should not be permitted to give thanks for food because an unregenerate person should not seek to pray was no doubt rather crass (and also reflects Williams's curious obsession with the act of prayer as being particularly decisive for a person's spiritual condition), but it reflects an inescapable Baptist concern that each person, including each child, has a pressing need to believe in Jesus. However sensitively it is handled, the individualistic strand of Baptist theology inevitably determines how Baptists understand the place of the child in the church, and so demands a more intensive focus on evangelism than is demanded of churches in other traditions, which are able to incorporate their children into the life of the church from their birth.

The place of the child, then, highlights the fact that the individualism that (I have argued) characterizes Baptist accounts of the Christian life intensifies the evangelistic imperative. This does not, however, directly explain the energy with which

Baptists have taken to the task of outreach beyond the local church fellowship, and indeed cross-cultural mission. While there are exceptions – the British General Baptists in the eighteenth century stand out as an extraordinarily insular group – Baptists through the ages and across the world have generally seemed to be extraordinarily committed to spreading (their understanding of) the gospel: Baptists were far from the only radical group to have representatives in Cromwell's Army, for instance, but they were the only group to leave multiple lasting congregations wherever the Army travelled. It is perhaps plausible to suppose that the heightened sense of the importance of spreading the gospel that the individualistic strand of Baptist theology offers simply becomes generalized; further, the distinctive Baptist hermeneutic of seeking to replicate New Testament ecclesial practice must inevitably tend towards a restless and wide-ranging missional engagement: most of the New Testament books, after all, are documents concerned with the furtherance of international mission programmes.

A Theology Shaped by Mission

I have suggested that there are some possible theological roots to the Baptist emphasis on mission; the next move is to ask how a focus on mission has shaped Baptist theology. A first place to look is sacramental theology: Baptist understandings, and practices, of baptism and Eucharist are distinctive, and missionally shaped. Both sacraments are commonly understood to be 'visual sermons', re-enactions of the core gospel narrative, visibly presenting the breaking of Christ's body, or the passage from death through burial to rebirth. I have noted already the rise, or rediscovery, of a more sacramental strand in Baptist theology in recent years; however, even on such an understanding there would be no denial of the visible witness to the gospel contained in the celebration of the sacraments, just an insistence that this is not all that is happening. Further, although there is no universal Baptist liturgy which may be interrogated, certain distinctive and common liturgical practices make clear this missional concern in Baptist sacramental theology.

Baptist practices of baptism of course stress the powerful visual impression created by the practice of full immersion; it will be clear to any observer that this practice is important in the life of this people, even if the observer understands nothing of what is going on. For this reason, it is very common for baptisms to be public events, either in the sense of a service within the usual sanctuary to which outsiders are particularly invited, or in the sense of a service which is taken out to beach, lakeside or riverbank, to be performed where it may be noticed by the passing public. The baptismal service will often be shaped with a particular concentration on outsiders who might come in: the choice of hymnody, the decoration of the church, the theme of the sermon and other aspects will all often be designed with the intention of being accessible and appealing to outsiders.

The common, if not universal, practice of having the baptismal candidate(s) give testimony to their experience of conversion, sometimes through the repetition of set formulae, but just as often through space being given in the service for their own account of their faith journey and the way they have known God's work in their lives, similarly points to the profoundly evangelistic intention of the baptismal service. Testimony is a long-recognized missional tool, which is deployed in classical manner, referred to and framed in the context of a presentation of the gospel in the sermon, in a Baptist baptismal service. The event is designed at every turn to be a presentation of the claims of Christ to those who are not yet believers. The sacrament is administered in a thoroughly missional manner.

Paul Fiddes has insightfully pointed out that Baptist Eucharistic liturgy is similarly missional. Baptists would baulk at the notion that the Eucharist is a 'converting ordinance' and so to be offered to unbelievers of good character, as was believed for a time in Congregational New England under the influence of Solomon Stoddard. Baptists fence the table – sometimes strictly; sometimes very loosely (the open communion position in British Baptist churches leads to an invitation being offered 'to all who love the Lord Jesus in sincerity and truth', or similar). That said, there are distinctive aspects of the way Baptists often celebrate the Eucharist that may be read as profoundly and deliberately missional. In particular, as Fiddes identified, Baptists traditionally recite the words of institution in proclamation, not in prayer. That is, in celebrating the Eucharist, Baptists declare Christ's central saving acts to the gathered congregation and to the world beyond, rather than recalling them before God.

The Baptist stress on evangelism has even affected accounts of theology proper; that is, of the life of God. Since the International Missionary Council meeting in Willlingen, Germany in 1952, it has been customary within ecumenical theology to speak of the *missio Dei*, the mission of God. The point of such language is to emphasize that the missionary task of the church (which, it should be said, has often been understood very broadly within the formalized ecumenical movement, often with an apparent attempt to minimize the role of personal evangelism) derives from the church's participation in the missionary purposes of God. It is not simply that the church has something to do; God has something to do, which the church is called – and sent – to participate in. The language can be traced at least as far back as Augustine, who (in the first half of *De Trinitate*) analyzed the 'missions' of the Son and Spirit, by which he meant their appearing in visible form within the created order to carry forward the divine plan of salvation. For Augustine, God's personal entrance into the created order was something anomalous and remarkable that stood in need of analysis and explanation; for contemporary theologians, by contrast, there is a tendency to assume that God's activity in the created realm is constitutive of who God is, and so that the divine missions are necessary to God's life.

An ambitious rhetorical development within European Baptist life led to a move from talking about 'the mission of God' to talking about 'the missionary God'. In one sense, in the context of the sorts of contemporary theological moves I have mentioned above, this appears unexceptional; the rhetorical force, however, is significant: talking of the church's (and the churches') participation in the *missio Dei*, the mission of God, at least implies a picture of God as the general, safely at home directing his troops into danger; or the sports coach on the sidelines, devising plans for her team to execute; God has a purpose, but sends the church to accomplish it. To move the language to speaking of God as missionary, however, pictures God as fully involved – the sergeant who leads the men into battle, or the captain who directs the team while playing a full part in the game herself. Of course, such analyses of rhetorical implication need to be used carefully: the meaning of a term is determined at least as much by its deployment as by the echoes it might carry, and many of those who spoke of the *missio Dei* (perhaps particularly Georg Vicedom) certainly used the term in the context of giving an account of God's full involvement in the mission.

That said, there is much power in finding language that speaks of God as actively involved, as not just standing at the gate waiting for the prodigal son to return, but wading purposefully through the mud of the pig-field in the far country to bring him assurances that he is still loved, even at his lowest point. However, is the picture theologically defensible? The obvious problem with the language is that, purely etymologically, 'missionary' necessarily implies 'being-sent', and it seems difficult to speak of God as being sent – who does the sending? Augustine's account of the Father's sending of the Son and Spirit is not really adequate; without getting too deeply involved in the sort of Trinitarian questions that were at the forefront of Augustine's mind, it still invites the image of the Father remotely waiting and directing. Better, perhaps, is an account inspired by Barth's insight that at the heart of the gospel is a daring belief that God determines to be God with and for human beings (and, we would now want to add, the rest of creation). God can be described as missionary in that, in sovereign freedom; God determines not just to be sent, but to send.

Baptist Contributions to Missiology

The emergence of the science of mission as a distinct subfield within theology is relatively recent: the academic contributions of Lesslie Newbigin, Andrew Walls and David Bosch (the last a Baptist) through the 1970s and 1980s might reasonably be seen as the first point at which missiology became a self-consciously distinct area of study. That said, once the academic discipline of 'missiology' is defined, it is easy to see Baptists in history who made a significant contribution to it: Fuller and Carey, of course; Oncken and Rauschenbusch also; the various partisans in the debates over the use of mission societies and Finney-like means in nineteenth-century America were engaged in a debate that we would now consider to be within the discipline of missiology.

Inevitably, many earlier missionaries made thoughtful contributions in this area: Bevan Jones's controversial text *The People of the Mosque* (1932) painted Islamic teaching as a kind of *praeparatio evangelica*, a teaching that made its followers more ready to hear and receive the gospel. Right or wrong, Jones was offering an early contribution to the theology of religions, and proposing a mode of dialogue and evangelism that, he felt, would be appropriate and effective for a particular people. This is classic missiology. (The recovery and examination of these earlier, practitioner-led, missiological insights is a task to which contemporary missiology has not given extensive attention; it may be that Baptists, with both a rich heritage in the area and a conviction that theology and practice belong together, should be developing a distinctive contribution here.)

David Bosch contributed widely to the development of missiology; there is little question, however, that his greatest work was *Transforming Mission: Paradigm Shifts in the Theology of Mission* (1991). In this book, Bosch borrowed the philosophical concept of 'paradigms', wide-ranging and incommensurate explanatory schemes offered to make sense of the variety of data in view. The book made clear how, in the New Testament as well as in later church history, different missiological paradigms come to prominence, leading to different practices of mission. Bosch's own experience as both a committed evangelical Baptist and an activist in the anti-apartheid movement in South Africa led him to propose that the coming effective missionary paradigm would be holistic, concerned with both gospel proclamation and the doing of justice, and seeing the two as intrinsically related.

Other Baptists who have made an outstanding contribution to missiology include several members of the Latin American Theological Fraternity, a group of scholars who sought on the one hand to find a distinctively evangelical expression of liberation theology, and on the other to challenge the control the West had over key missiological bodies, particularly the Lausanne Congress. Orlando Costas, Samuel Escobar and René Padilla are among the Baptists who stand out in this context, with Costas, despite his early death, perhaps being the most significant intellectually. For Costas, God's preferential option to the poor was a given datum of Scripture, which needed to reshape evangelical missional practice, without, however, any loss of the centrality of gospel proclamation. Costas himself was acutely aware of the ways in which the social and intellectual context a person inhabited shaped and determined their understanding of theological questions, and indeed was particularly conscious of this dynamic at play in his own life. As he experienced different local situations, his thought deepened and broadened, and he was extremely open about the new perspectives and challenges that he found in each new context and about his attempts to integrate them into his broader thought.

It is difficult, however, to find very much that is distinctively Baptist about the thought of Bosch or Costas (Bosch, to be fair, developed an account of the missional impact of the countercultural believers' church, but this aspect of his thinking has been far less influential, indeed far less noticed, than the less distinctively Baptist themes noted above). It is striking, and perhaps indicative of the identity of the tradition, that Baptists seem to have produced a disproportionately large number of world-leading missiologists, while producing disproportionately low numbers of scholars in other theological disciplines; Baptists missiologists do not, however, seem to have yet developed a distinctively Baptist missiology. In hearing the call to make disciples, Baptists have been committed to the work of mission, and (in some cases) have thought long and deeply about it; it seems difficult, however, to argue that their conclusions have been very different from those of other evangelical thinkers.

Discipleship and Holiness

The call to make disciples goes beyond evangelism to the nurture of Christians so that they are mature. In Baptist understanding, Christian maturity has two particular foci: playing a full part in the work of the local church, as earlier discussed; and growing in ethical purity, in holiness. In the fine old phrase, a Baptist church is a covenanted congregation of visible saints, walking together in the ways of the Lord and watching over one another. Each clause of this definition bears reflection.

To start in the middle, the notion of 'visible saints' is not a claim to perfection: the belief in the possibility of attaining 'Christian perfection' in this life is a Methodist distinctive, not a Baptist one, and not one that has ever found significant purchase in Baptist life, to the best of my knowledge. (The most likely contexts would seem to be eighteenth-century Baptist movements that have a demonstrable link to the Wesleyan branch of the Evangelical Revival, such as the New Connexion of General Baptists, but there is no evidence here that entire sanctification was entertained or taught.) Instead, there is at least an expectation that those who are members of a Baptist church will display visibly higher standards of ethics than those around them; and that they will be open to correction, and committed to repentance and the amendment of their lives when correction comes (more on this below). There is also often an (informal) list of public behaviours that are unacceptable and assumed to be avoidable: at times this has included the use of tobacco and/or alcohol; working on the Sabbath; participation in the slave trade; attending the theatre; marrying a non-Baptist; and even the registering of a patent (an admittedly obscure case in seventeenth-century English General Baptist life).

This third point might be found troubling in two ways: first, does it propose a two-level theory of sin, in which pride (for instance) might be rebuked, but Sunday trading would lead to exclusion from the church? Two things should be said in response, the first being that there was and is generally an opportunity for repentance, unless the fault has become regular and habitual. Second, however, the records of church discipline often contain the sense that certain acts, by their deliberate and extended nature, can be assumed to involve a deliberate and planned flaunting of the church's standards. One might surrender to pride, anger or indeed lust, in the face of a moment's temptation; this is not acceptable, but it is perhaps understandable. To open one's shop on a Sunday, however, is not the result of a moment's moral weakness; it is an extended and deliberate act; similarly for marriage outside of the Baptist community, or attending the theatre.

These last two examples, however, raise the second troubling aspect of the list: are these really such grave sins as to merit exclusion from the church community? The first Baptist response would be to refuse the premise implied in the question: any sin, if obstinately maintained in the face of church censure, merits exclusion from the church community, because any obstinate sinning is a straightforward refusal to bend the knee before King Jesus. It may be that his prohibition of idolatry is in some important sense more significant than his prohibition of patent-holding (assuming, for the sake of the argument, that this is in fact his prohibition, and not, as seems likely, an eccentric misapprehension on the part of a church): to knowingly and deliberately flaunt either prohibition, however, is equally to refuse to obey the King's commands. Treason in seemingly minor matters remains treason.

That said, a second response must be made: there is no authorized list of such forbidden practices; each church has liberty to interpret Christ's command. Culture and context is important: in contemporary cultures, while particular productions might require sober discernment, the theatre is a serious art form that contributes not just aesthetically, but also to the crucial debates of the day; it may be that the theatre in a particular time and place uniformly offered little more than coarse humour and titillation, in which case a blanket ban on the theatre may have been appropriate. There is little question that the urgency of the nineteenth-century temperance movement, to change the example, stemmed from the central role drunkenness played in many of the crucial social evils of the day: domestic and street violence, child malnutrition and poverty and so on. In context, temperance can be seen as a prophetic response to the particular society and one that should be honoured, if perhaps not aped. It is the high and holy task of each Baptist congregation at each particular point in its story to discern what socially accepted practices it should take a stand against; if sometimes congregations, individually or *en masse*, have failed (either in the direction of tolerating a true social evil, or in the direction of an inappropriate moralism), that does not mean that it is wrong for congregations to believe they are called to this task.

Baptist churches, then, will expect not just conformity on some social issues, but in general a visibly higher standard of life than the society around them, and will expect members to be ready to repent and change if confronted with evidence of their failure to live up to their high calling to be visible saints. An examination of Baptist practice suggests that there are three basic reasons for falling into sin, 'through ignorance, through weakness, through our own deliberate fault' as a liturgy hated by early Baptists had it. The 'deliberate fault' clause has been dealt with in the discussion above; ignorance and weakness remain.

There will be times when a believer is unaware that this or that behaviour is perceived, by their church fellowship, to be unacceptable. The proper response at this point is challenge, instruction and so edification. The believer is to be guided into a more adequate understanding of Christ's call on their life by their sisters and brothers. (The strange patent case I referred to above began with a private suggestion that the behaviour of the brother who took out the patent was unethical, because tantamount to an immoderate love of money; when he refused to accept this rebuke the matter was brought to the church meeting and the censure there confirmed and repeated; only when he refused the censure of the church was he excommunicated. After that, the spat became somewhat ugly, with appeals to the broader denomination and a pamphlet war.) In an ideal situation, of course, every disciple would be fully briefed on ethical questions before he or she had the opportunity to offend; in reality, teaching may be delayed or incomplete, or the occasion of sin may arise so quickly that there has been no time for instruction, or a completely new context which demands reflection on the part of the church may come into being, or a church may become convinced that practices previously regarded as unexceptional should now be censured. In all these situations, instruction will follow, rather than proceed, a sinful act, with the intention that the brother repent of his failing, and resolve not to fail similarly again.

Weakness is another context again. The sister who knows that anger is wrong or who has struggled with pride may nonetheless find anger flaring up within her heart, or find herself responding with pride when her achievements are praised in public. This is the point where the Baptist denial of perfectionism becomes relevant: all fall from time to time; in God's good mercy, and because of what Jesus has done, forgiveness and restoration is available to all who repent. Baptists do not believe that they are perfect; but they do believe that, in Christ, they are forgiven for their failures, and that, in the Spirit, they can and must strive to be better than they have been.

Walking together: Corporate Holiness

'Visible saints, walking together in the ways of the Lord and watching over each other': this definition of holiness is irreducibly corporate. Specifically, Baptists find sanctification within the community of the local church and not elsewhere.

Within the Christian tradition this is unusual, if not eccentric. Normative sanctity seems to involve withdrawal from community, not immersion in it: saints withdrew into the desert, or up mountains, or into separated cells, there to pursue holiness freed from the distractions and temptations afforded by a surrounding community. While this was somewhat regulated within the monastic tradition, which at least proposed community living, practices of silence and withdrawal still seemed to suggest that human contact was an impediment to the pursuit of the holy life. The only significant relationships were with spiritual directors, who served to interpret and guide the endless and varied impulses of the heart in the right directions.

For Baptists, spiritual direction is an irreducibly communal activity, performed by the whole church for each member of the church, and insertion into the community of God's people is not an impediment, but a necessary spur to true holiness.; that is, Baptists 'watch over' one another, and 'walk *together* in the ways of the Lord'. It would not be wrong to read the first part of this as a result of the Baptist rejection of clericalism, but it is a particular, and far from inevitable, response to that rejection. Certainly, Baptists have always refused the notion that the Christian needs any intermediary to relate to God – this is what I have termed the individualistic strand in Baptist theology. One could respond to this idea, of course, with a very individualistic spirituality in which all human communities are rejected to seek God alone in whatever way seems appropriate or helpful. This has never been the Baptist way. God, for Baptists, is encountered and known in a gathered community and, indeed, by a gathered community; the lone believer is at least profoundly disadvantaged in his or her discipleship.

Rejecting clericalism, then, Baptists have substituted a community. The mind of Christ is known, not through the diktats of some supposedly privileged interpreter, but by God's people gathered together. For a Baptist, all fellow-members of the local church share a responsibility to examine his or her walk, to nurture and instruct him and to help him or her grow in grace. We seek guidance on progress in discipleship and growth in holiness not by seeking out a heroic sensei, but by coming together and trusting that Christ, by his Spirit, can and will speak to us and through us. Baptists guide and disciple one another, under the rule of Christ.

This is not quite unique in the Christian tradition, for instance, the early Methodist class-meeting was supposed to work in much the same way, and there is some resonance with the base communities described by contemporary Latin American liberation theologians. It is, however, both profoundly difficult to live out and radical in its implications. Whatever social hierarchies we have established are subverted by this Baptist practice: the believer, secure in their worldly status, is potentially required to take instruction, humbly and reverently, from social inferiors or children or employees or those of lower caste or those of limited education or people with disabilities or women or people of supposedly inferior ethnic backgrounds. When God's Spirit is poured out on slaves, male and female, when sons and daughters prophesy, when old people see visions and young people dream dreams, and every member of the church community is called to take each contribution with utmost seriousness as being part of the way in which Christ's mind is known, some extraordinarily serious political reconfigurations are taking place,[3] and that will be profoundly painful to those who – like me – who have enjoyed the happy accident of being born on the 'right' side of most or all political inequalities.

The sheer radicalness of Baptist spirituality does not stop there, however: so far, this is an account of saints 'watching over' one another; the Baptist tradition also insists that visible saints are 'walking together'. Holiness of life is irreducibly communal. I cannot follow Jesus without being part of a community that is following Jesus. The local church fellowship achieves a measure of holiness together or not at all.

It is tempting, and probably not inappropriate, to narrate this is in terms of some recent theological and philosophical theory which has begun to recognize the ethical and epistemological significance of immersion in a community; the early Baptists, however, were not thinking in terms of post-liberal analysis or of MacIntyrian-traditioned communities. For them, the core and simple fact was that Christ was present and known in gathered community, and not otherwise. Faced with a question concerning appropriate behaviour for a disciple of Jesus, the Baptist's only recourse for an answer is the local church community. Outside of a local church community, ignorance and confusion are normal and inevitable. The community does not guarantee the holy lives of its members, but it does make them possible – it is a necessary condition for personal holiness, if not a sufficient one.

Of course, 'walking together' and 'watching over' are related realities. The fact that the disciple's sisters and brothers are faithful to God's calling on their lives, to watch over his or her life, enables him or her to walk well before God. Loving community discipline enables the discipleship of every member of the community; members of the community share insight and encouragement, pray for one another, step in to challenge or uphold one another, and in manifold ways, make joint discipleship possible where individual discipleship is not. For Baptists, sanctity happens together or not at all, and this belief sets us apart from most other Christian communities in far-reaching ways.

Togetherness, community, is not something that happens by accident for Baptists, however. Church is necessarily intentional. In my initial definition of the Baptist church, the key phrase is 'covenanted community'. At a simple level, this speaks merely of a degree of permanence and intentionality: the Baptist church is not a happenstance of pilgrims meeting together in an inn on the way to Canterbury (for instance), but something that happens when a group of Christians choose, in obedience to Christ's call, to invest their lives in one another. This is what is implied in the term 'covenanted community'. The concept of 'covenant' has recently returned to prominence in some areas of Baptist theology and deserves some consideration here.

The Baptist movement began as the federal theology of seventeenth-century Calvinism was developing; this tradition understood God's dealings with humanity to be regulated according to a series of covenants, each established sovereignly by God, and each specifying God's gracious provision for the people, and

God's requirements of the people. A 'covenant of works' made with Adam and Eve promised divine presence, provision and blessing on the condition of obedience to the primitive law – the command not to eat of the fruit of the tree of knowledge of good and evil. When this covenant was breached, God made a new covenant, the 'covenant of grace', under which God sent the Messiah, Jesus, into the world, and which promised that all who believe in the Messiah would have their sins forgiven and would be received as adopted children of God at the final resurrection. (There are various developments and nuances of this basic scheme, but they are not significant here.)

Coupled with this was a more local use of the word 'covenant', which itself had a twofold reference. It was common to speak of a local church covenant, which was, on the one hand, God's corporate promise to the church (borrowing language from God's dealings with Israel, 'I will be your people, and you will be my God'), and on the other, the promise made between believers within the church to walk together and watch over one another. Early English Baptist theology fused this local use with the covenant of grace: the application of God's promise of redemption is in the formation of the local church covenant. This is a striking elevation of the role of the local church, albeit entirely consonant with the ecclesiology I have so far described. Salvation – sharing in the covenant of grace – is only achieved through participation in a local covenant within a local church. To put it plainly, unless I am promised with other believers to seek to walk together and to watch over one another, I have no share in the salvation Christ won at Calvary.

On this understanding, the 'covenanted community' is not a trivial or dispensable organization; it is precisely and the only context in which the salvation God has made available and actual in Christ is appropriated. John Smyth, the first founder of the Baptist movement, described 'the visible church of Christ' as 'the chief and principle part of the gospel'; salvation happens within, and not without, local churches that are pledged to watch over one another and to follow to the way of Christ as best they understand it. God's promises of grace become real not primarily in individual lives, but in the life of a community of promise that has responded to what God has given by coming together to make its own promises before God.

This, it seems to me, is a stirring but radical interpretation of Baptist theology which elevates the classical Baptist stress on the local congregation to a remarkably high level. It is, at present, very much a minority report within Baptist theology, but claims to be retrieving themes from the origins of the movement, and so needs to be taken with some degree of seriousness. That said, it is possible to offer a Baptist theology which is adequately serious about the place of the local gathered church in soteriology, but which does not travel the radical root of this Baptist covenantalism.

Baptist Visions of Christian Ethics

In all this talk of holiness, is there a distinctive Baptist account of what the well-lived Christian life looks like? The question is not easy: there are those who would insist that there is, in some cases, locating the practice of non-violence at the heart of things; there are others who would struggle to see any Baptist ethics that was not also evangelical ethics: after all, we share convictions and a source of authority with non-Baptist evangelicals.

The argument for a distinctive position is fairly easy to sketch: at the heart of the Baptist vision of what it is to be the church is a belief in the non-coercion of belief; violence is inevitably an act of coercion, therefore to be a Baptist is to reject violence. Thus stated, the potential logical problem in the argument is also clear: can a commitment to non-coercion in matters of belief (which is unquestionably Baptist) be extended legitimately to a commitment to non-coercion in all matters? Clearly, without further argument, this move is a problem, but further argument is available, relying on a general account of the way of Christ or of life in the Kingdom as being non-coercive. On this basis, the argument is rendered plausible, and more 'Anabaptist' strands of the Baptist tradition would find it compelling. Baptist ethics then finds a central principle in non-coercion, or pacifism, and are, if not distinctive, at least aligned with what is very much a minority report from peace church traditions.

More 'Reformed' strands of the Baptist tradition would accept the point about non-coercion in matters of belief (and religious practice), but would reject the idea that this can be extended more generally. It is appropriate to apply coercive punishments to lawbreakers, for instance; so long as the law is just, this is not a trespassing into the realm that Christ the King claims as his own; rather it is an appropriate and Godly application of justice in the realm that God grants to the civil magistrate to administer. Baptist ethics is not based on pacifism, or indeed committed to that position; in fact, with certain clear but limited differences around the question of the relationships of state and church, and of minister and members, Baptist ethics is basically the same as other evangelical and Reformed ethics.

I would argue that Baptist ethics has only one crucial distinctive position which can never be compromised or surrendered – the claim that, as I put it in the previous chapter, 'Christ is Lord, and the believer is free'. In a modern pluralist and liberal democracy, it might be that freedom of religion is sufficiently protected in law that this distinctive appears to be not at all distinct; at the very least, however, the reason for arriving at it – a confession of the immediate Lordship of Christ – is profoundly different from general defences of pluralism in a liberal democracy; the evidence suggests, however, that most contemporary societies are extraordinarily chary of this position, and that a robust and principled witness for the freedom of all to worship as their consciences shall lead remains, at best, a fragile freedom that stands in constant need of defence.

Conclusion

A Vision of Baptist Theology

I began this book suggesting that any account of Baptist theology would inevitably be partial and creative, simply because the tradition does not have a long and settled history of reflection on its own doctrinal identity. I have chosen to emphasize the immediate Lordship of Christ over every individual human person and over every particular gathered church. I have offered expositions of central Baptist distinctives on this basis, attempting to demonstrate that stressing these two foci can give unity and support to various historically identified Baptist distinctives. In beginning the book with brief historical accounts of the developments within Baptist thought, I hope to have given enough context to show that my proposal is able to narrate sensibly many, perhaps most, of the variety of traditions and positions that can be considered Baptist through history.

That said, I do not pretend, of course, to have solved the question of Baptist identity; indeed I suspect that the question will not be solved for some while: the process we must go through would seem to involve the gathering of a number of tentative proposals such as this one, and their development, defence and refinement by several hands. When we have several 'schools' of Baptist theology, each actively engaged in exploring its own validity historically, and in displaying its own potential for being a source of vitality, vision and renewal within the churches, then we may hope for a mature scholarly engagement between those different schools, which will leave us with a clear map of possible visions of Baptist identity.

Is the effort worth it? I believe it is: when Smyth baptized himself, and then Helwys, four centuries ago, a movement began that for all its faults and false turns and foibles, has proved repeatedly generative and dynamic. It has spread across the world and inspired heroic evangelistic efforts and magnificent campaigns for justice;

it has spoken peace to broken sinners and convinced those most despised by society of their true worth in the eyes of God. It has given us, too, its own iconic moments, pictures of the ways in which a vision can enable the faithful believer to see the possibilities undreamt of by anyone else, and, with the holy boldness that only the Spirit of God can give, to dare to pursue them.

When Roger Williams insisted that a woman could and must follow her own conscience, and not be beaten into submission by her husband; when William Carey suggested that the gospel should be preached across the whole world; when Martin Luther King believed enough in the dignity of every human being to propose a strategy of non-violent resistance to demand civil rights – in each case something significant happened, and it was made to happen by people who were living out a vision of how to follow God, a vision which seemed to enable them, and countless millions of other believers, women and men, young and old, from almost every nation on earth, to dare to believe that the call of Christ could lift up the despised, lead sinners to repentance, forgiveness and holiness of life and successfully challenge injustice. It was and is a vision found in the Bible, but in a particular way of grasping the Bible – others coming equally seriously to the same text, could support the social order instead of challenging it, or rest easy that the missionary task was not as urgent as it may appear. To attempt the work of narrating Baptist theology is to attempt the work of identifying that particular way of grasping the Bible.

It is more than that, though. It is also to attempt a work of purification: it is to try to identify the places where we have failed to be faithful enough to the biblical call, to try to spot distortions that leave us conforming to the world, not to the vision of Christ-like living. If we can better narrate the Baptist vision, we can better perform this work of diagnosis. The task will never be done perfectly, but that is not a reason to shy away from it. I dare to believe that the Baptist vision is something sufficiently and profoundly right that, if only we could get an adequately clear sight of it, I would feel able to say, as Gambrell once did, 'I am a Baptist . . . and all the world ought to be.'

Notes

Introduction

1 Recognizing, of course, that Arminian theology, although repudiated by the Reformed tradition, was itself an off-shoot of that tradition (Arminius studied under Beza, after all) and so that the Arminian beliefs of the first Baptists are not a problem for this position.
2 L. Russ Bush, and Tom J. Nettles, *Baptists and the Bible (Revised and Expanded Edition)* (Nashville: Broadman & Holman, 1999), p. xvii.
3 I am of course aware of the negative connotations of 'individual' and 'individualism' in some contemporary theology, and indeed choose the word partly for its rhetorical force. I defend my use in conversation with some recent discussions in Chapter 5 below.
4 To illustrate, there is presently some agitation within British churches concerning a law proposing the repeal of a ban on the celebration of same-sex civil partnerships on religious premises; for Baptists, the point is simply trivial: the civil law has no business banning any form of religious celebration, and so no business banning this one. I suppose that (almost?) every British Baptist church would refuse to allow its premises to be used for the purpose specified, but this, in Baptist polity, has to be the decision of the church, not a ruling imposed by the government. Baptists will argue the legal point in a different way to Presbyterians or Anglicans, who assume the right of the government to make laws concerning worship.
5 This line was attributed to Gambrell by his friend H. Boyce Taylor and has been reproduced in various places since. I am grateful to Pastor Ben Stratton (personal communication) for this information.

Chapter 1

1 Quoted in Bill J. Leonard, *The Challenge of Being Baptist: Owning a scandalous past and an uncertain future* (Waco, TX: Baylor UP, 2010), p. 15.
2 From Henry's address to the Speaker of the House of Commons, 11th May, 1532, quoted in A.G. Dickens, The English Reformation (London: Collins, 1967).
3 From the 'Preface' to the 1550 Ordinal; the text was preserved, with only minor changes of spelling, into the 1662 *Book of Common Prayer*.
4 B. R. White, The English Baptists of the 17th Century (London: Baptist Historical Society, 1983), p. 24.

5 W. T. Whitley, *A History of British Baptists* (London: Charles Griffen, 1923), p. 53.
6 A. C. Underwood, *A History of the English Baptists* (London: Carey Kingsgate, 1947), p. 116.
7 Raymond Brown, *The English Baptists of the Eighteenth Century* (London: Baptist Historical Society, 1986), p. 16.
8 David W. Bebbington, *Baptists Through the Centuries: A history of a global people* (Waco, TX: Baylor UP, 2010), p. 75.
9 Earnest A. Payne, *The Baptist Union: A Short History* (London: BUGB, 1958), p. 267.
10 Bebbington, *Baptists through the Centuries*, pp. 70–1.

Chapter 2

1 This is the burden of several of Edwards's works, culminating in his *Treatise on the Religious Affections* (1746); for some analysis of the point, see my '*Religious Affections* by Jonathan Edwards' in Kelly Kapic and Randal Gleason (eds), *The Devoted Life: An invitation to the Puritan classics* (Downers Grove, IL: IVP, 2004), pp. 285–97.
2 The text was printed in *Signs of the Times*, 23 November 1832. It is available on several websites.
3 See Bebbington, *Baptists Through the Centuries*, pp. 88–9.
4 Figures from 'Primitive Baptists' in William H. Brackney, *An A–Z of the Baptists* (Lanham: Scarecrow Press, 2009), p. 457.
5 The division of the denomination on racial lines which happened after the Civil War largely persists; Brackney, *A–Z*, gives 1700 churches and 64,000 members as of 1995 for the white Primitives, and 500 congregations with 50,000 members as of 2005 for the black Primitive Baptists.
6 William H. Brackney, *Baptists in North America* (Oxford: Blackwell, 2006), p. 65.
7 And worse; active membership of the Ku Klux Klan was not, for example, regarded as incompatible with membership, and even office holding, in Southern Baptist churches. See Paul Harvey, *Freedom's Coming: Religious Culture and the Shaping of the American South from the Civil War through the Civil Rights Era* (Chapel Hill: University of North Carolina Press, 2005).
8 Dixon had attacked Harper himself, in 1891, alleging that he had claimed the existence of errors in Isaiah.
9 The best current edition is George M. Marsden (ed.), *The Fundamentals: A Testimony to the Truth* (12 vols in 4) (New York: Garland, 1988).
10 The first volume opened with essays by James Orr, B. B. Warfield and G. Campbell Morgan; H. C. G. Moule contributed to the second; for the Baptists, E. Y. Mullins contributed to the third volume.
11 See, for instance, James Orr on 'The Early Narratives of Genesis' in vol. VI. George Marsden notes that *The Fundamentals* 'represent the movement

[*sic*, fundamentalism] at a moderate and transitional stage, before it was reshaped and pushed to extremes by the intense heat of controversy.' *Fundamentalism and American Culture: The Shaping of Twentieth-Century Evangelicalism, 1870–1925* (Oxford: OUP, 1980), p. 119.

12 George M. Marsden, Fundamentalism and American Culture (Oxford: OUP, 2006), p. 235.

Chapter 3

1 *Metropolitan Tabernacle Pulpit* X (1864), p. 317. It is difficult to resist Spurgeon's point; in the liturgy, immediately after the act of baptism, the priest declares 'Seeing now, dearly beloved brethren, that this Child is regenerate and grafted into the body of Christ's Church'. *BCP* (1662), 'Public Baptism of Infants'.

2 From the Baptist Times of 19th April 1918, quoted in Randall, The English Baptists of the 20th Century, p. 104.

3 See C. McDaniel & R. V. Pierard, 'The Politics of Appointments to Protestant Theological Faculties in Germany: The Case of Professor Erich Geldbach', *Journal of Church & State* 46 (2004), 55–82.

Chapter 4

1 I have an essay in preparation on Caffyn; at present I do not think any published source does justice to his views, as contemporary sources are all partial in one direction or the other, and all later historians repeat as fact charges of heresy that seem to me to be, in some cases, demonstrably wrong, and in others, at best, unproven.

2 Full publication details of all texts referred to in this chapter will be found in the Bibliography at the end of this book; to avoid a proliferation of footnotes, I will only reference direct quotations here.

3 For a helpful guide to the debate – and from a Baptist – see Millard J. Erickson, *Who's Tampering with the Trinity: An assessment of the subordination debate* (Grand Rapids: Kregel, 2009).

Chapter 5

1 There is some resistance to the use of the word 'sacrament' in Baptist theology, both historically and in the present day. 'Ordinance' is held to be safer, as pointing simply to the origin of Baptism and the Lord's Supper in the command of Jesus. It seems to me that there is nothing inherently problematic in the term 'sacrament' (its etymology locates the practices it describes as visible signs or seals of Christian identity, which is hardly

objectionable); if in some contexts it carries such baggage that it needs to be avoided, that is understandable, but there is value in using ecumenically accessible terms where we can.

2 *Pushing at the Boundaries of Unity: Anglicans and Baptists in Conversation* (London: Church House Publishing, 2005), p. 73. The present author was a member of the group that prepared this report.

3 George R. Beasley-Murray, *Baptism in the New Testament* (Grand Rapids: Eerdmans, 1962).

4 Equally it has been argued that the rise of the symbolic understanding of baptism (and the Eucharist) owed much to rationalist ways of thought in the eighteenth century, and to a suspicion that any 'supernaturalist' view was akin to Roman Catholicism in the context of opposition to the rise of Anglo-Catholicism in the early nineteenth century. See Horton Davies, *Worship and Theology in England: From Watts and Wesley to Martineau, 1690–1900* (Grand Rapids: Eerdmans, 1996), vol. IV, pp. 83–4.

5 On this, see variously my Whitley Lecture, *Tradition and Renewal in Baptist Life* (Oxford: Whitley, 2003); Philip E. Thompson, 'Towards Baptist Ecclesiology in Pneumatological Perspective' (PhD Thesis, Emory University, 2005); Anthony R. Cross & Philip E. Thompson (eds) *Baptist Sacramentalism* (Carlisle: Paternoster, 2003); *idem*, *Baptist Sacramentalism 2* (Carlisle: Paternoster, 2008); Steven R. Harmon, *Towards Baptist Catholicity: Essays on Tradition and the Baptist Vision* (Carlisle: Paternoster, 2006).

6 John D. Zizioulas, *Being as Communion: Studies in Personhood and the Church* (London: DLT, 1985), pp. 49–65.

7 *Baptism, Eucharist and Ministry* (Geneva: World Council of Churches, 1982.

8 Although the 1678 'Orthodox Creed' of the English General Baptists included the text, and the inaugural meeting of the Baptist World Alliance in 1905 began with a recitation of the Creed. For an argument that the Creed might nonetheless be received as authoritative by one committed to the position that Scripture alone has authority, see my *Listening to the Past: The Place of Tradition in Theology* (Carlisle: Paternoster, 2002), pp. 153–64.

9 The British Baptists who accepted the terms of the 1689 Act of Toleration in fact affirmed their belief in the Nicene Creed through this acceptance, as the Act required subscription to the Anglican Articles of Religion, with certain limited exceptions; this included subscription to Article VIII, which affirms the conformity of the 'three creeds' (Apostles', Nicene and Athanasian) with Scripture.

10 The *Baptist Faith and Message*, the primary confessional document of the Southern Baptist Convention, has described Baptist churches as operating 'through democratic processes' in both its 1963 revision and the current (2000) revision. Such wording makes the polity luminously clear, but does seem in danger of inviting confusion between current cultural/political preferences and a theological claim about Christ's lordship.

11 B. R. White (ed.), *Association Records of the Particular Baptists of England, Wales, and Ireland to 1660* (London: Baptist Historical Society, 1971), p. 126.

12 Elliott Smith, *The Advance of Baptist Associations across America*, (Nashville,TN: Broadman Press, 1979) p. 23.
13 Prokhanov confession; trans. from Lumpkin, p. 427.
14 *Baptism, Eucharist and Ministry* (Faith & Order Paper 111; Geneva: World Council of Churches, 1982), M.II.7, p. 21.
15 Paul Goodliff, *Ministry, Sacrament and Representation: Ministry and Ordination in Contemporary Baptist Theology, and the Rise of Sacramentalism* (Oxford: Regent's Park College, 2010).
16 Robert E. Johnson, *A Global Introduction to Baptist Churches* (Cambridge: CUP, 2010), pp. 231–2.

Chapter 6

1 I quote a modern edition, with updated spellings here: Joe Early, Jr, *The Life and Writings of Thomas Helwys* (Early English Baptist Texts) (Macon, GA: Mercer UP, 2009). The *Short Declaration* can be found on pp.155–310.
2 Text from Brian Haymes, 'Thomas Helwys' *The Mystery of Iniquity*: Is it still Relevant in the Twenty-First Century?' in Anthony R. Cross & Nicholas J. Wood (eds), *Exploring Baptist Origins* (Oxford: Regent's Park College, 2010), pp. 61–77; text on p. 64, and reproduction of inscription on p. 77.
3 There are modern editions; I have, however, resorted to the original. Roger Williams, *The Bloudy Tenent of Persecution. . .* (London: *s.n.*, 1644).
4 See Joseph L. Blau, 'The Wall of Separation', *Union Seminary Quarterly Review* 38 (1984), 263–88, 263–7 for some details of sources.
5 On this see Ellis M. West, 'Roger Williams on the limits of religious liberty' *Annual of the Society of Christian Ethics* 1988, 133–60, especially 139–41.
6 See West, 'Roger Williams on the limits of religious liberty', pp. 145–7, for details of this case.
7 Stanley Grenz's *Isaac Backus: Puritan and Baptist* (Macon, GA: Mercer UP, 1983) is excellent an general guide to Backus. On his account of liberty of conscience, see pp. 150–80. I find Grenz's account wholly convincing, and am following his interpretations here.
8 From a published letter of 1771; quoted in Grenz, *Isaac Backus* p. 154.
9 Both quotations from the 1768 'Petition' of the Ashfield Baptists to the General Court.
10 James Ernst, quoted in McBeth, *Baptist Heritage*, p. 130.
11 See Keith G. Jones, *The European Baptist Federation: A Case Study in European Baptist Interdependency 1950–2006* (*SBHT* 43) (Milton Keynes: Paternoster, 2009), pp. 257–9, and Toivo Pilli, 'Baptist Identities in Eastern Europe' in Ian M. Randall, Toivo Pilli, and Anthony R. Cross (eds) *Baptist Identities: International Studies from the Seventeenth to the Twentieth Centuries* (*SBHT* 19) (Milton Keynes: Paternoster, 2006), pp. 92–108 and pp. 104–6, for some examples of this.

12 E.Y. Mullins, *The Axioms of Religion: A New Interpretation of the Baptist Faith* (Philadelphia: American Baptist Publications Society, 1908).

13 See, e.g., H. Wheeler Robinson, *The Life and Faith of the Baptists* (London: Kingsgate, 1946), pp. 142–3.

14 Opening words of the 1939 'Text of the Declaration of Religious Liberty adopted. . .' in Henry Cook, *What Baptists Stand For* (London: Carey Kingsgate, 1964[5]), pp. 248–9.

15 Arnold Theodore Ohrn, who in 1950 in lectures in Southwestern Seminary suggested that the kingship of Christ should be the key theme. (This is reported by Garrett, Baptist Theology, p. 427, citing unpublished manuscripts.)

16 'Torture – uniquely terrible', BWA < http://www.bwanet.org/bwa.php?m=news&p=news_item&id=498 > accessed 28 June 2011.

17 Wright's views have been developed over many publications, but perhaps the single best source is Nigel G. Wright, *Free Church, Free State : The Positive Baptist Vision* (Milton Keynes: Paternoster, 2005).

18 Both quotations from Wright, *Free Church*, p. 213.

19 Wright, *Free Church*, p. 218.

Chapter 7

1 McBeth, *Baptist Heritage*, p. 470. There is, unfortunately, very little serious work on Oncken and his mission available in English. H. Luckley, *J. G. Oncken und die Anflänge des deutschen Baptismus* (Kassel: Oncken Verlag, 1934) remains the best source in German.

2 Quoted in Keith G. Jones, *The European Baptist Federation*, p. 16.

3 In passing, this relates back to the point I made about the incompatibility of Baptist ecclesiology with arguments that propose authority in the church is limited to men only; in a Baptist church, 'visible saints watch over each other'; authority is thus necessarily distributed among all members.

Bibliography

Works on Baptist Theology

Because of the introductory nature of the series of which this volume is a part, I have not provided extensive documentation of my claims, or any discussion of the secondary literature. Here, I offer some annotated guidance for those wishing to explore further. As noted above, there is not really a discipline of 'Baptist theology'; there are, however, some useful reference works and a few other personal visions of what the discipline looks like.

Any consideration of Baptist theology needs to have a place for the foundational confessions of the seventeenth century and for those confessional materials that have been produced from time to time since then. William Lumpkin's *Baptist Confessions of Faith* remains the best single source (full bibliographic details of all works cited are in the list below), and is good on the British and US traditions; Lumpkin has some more international sources, but a work with a more global focus is sorely needed.

William H. Brackney has provided much useful historical material on Baptist thought in a number of works spread over a distinguished career. Of particular note here are his *Genetic History of Baptist Thought*, and his *A to Z of the Baptists*, which is a helpful encyclopedic guide. The subtitle of the former specifies its focus on 'Britain and North America'; the *A to Z* attempts a more international focus. For the student interested in non-Anglophone Baptist life, John H. Y. Briggs, *A Dictionary of European Baptist Life and Thought* is an important window to the disparate Baptist traditions of greater Europe; the balance of its entries is less towards the biographical and more towards the thematic than Brackney's *A to Z*, which makes it both a useful complement, and of particular interest to the student of theology rather than history.

In listing reference works, James Leo Garrett's massive *Baptist Theology: A four-century study* must be included. In over 700 pages it seeks to tell the story of Baptist theology through a series of sketches of significant individuals, roughly in chronological order. The choice of those included appears biased, not just towards the US, but towards those who were active in certain denominational institutions within the US; and Garrett's ready willingness to measure all his subjects up against a particular theological rule and thus to pronounce on their orthodoxy can become grating; that said, he is generally fair in his account of what this or that writer did teach, even if sometimes harsh in judging its worth; and, for the tradition he covers, the student of Baptist theology will find nothing even approaching this work in comprehensiveness.

I have noted myself the lack of primary material for Baptist theology beyond the West; the series of papers arising from the meetings of the International

Conference on Baptist Studies are thus of great importance in beginning, at least, to provide scholarly access to the diverse and fascinating Baptist traditions of the Majority World. Three volumes have appeared in the Paternoster *Studies in Baptist History and Thought* series: *The Gospel in the World* (ed. Bebbington), *Baptist Identities* (ed. Randall, Pilli and Cross) and *Baptists and Mission* (ed. Randall and Cross); the papers from the second conference appeared in a special issue of *Baptist History and Heritage* (vol. XXXVI.1–2 [2001]). Further contributions are eagerly awaited.

Recent attempts to give an account of a specifically Baptist vision of theology include: Bill J. Leonard's *The Challenge of Being Baptist*, Paul S. Fiddes's *Tracks and Traces* and a vision developed by Nigel Wright in various places, but particularly *New Baptists, New Agenda* and *Free Church: Free State* (see also a Festschrift exploring Wright's theology: Lalleman [ed.], *Challenging to Change*). Beyond these few examples, we find theologies that are perhaps influenced by their author's Baptist tradition (Grenz's *Theology for the Community of God* would be a fine example), but which are not particularly attempts to write a Baptist theology.

Works on Baptist History

Baptists fare better when it comes to analyses of their history. Indeed, from Backus and Crosby in the eighteenth century down to the present, Baptists have consistently produced outstanding and sympathetic historians from their own ranks. At present, the standard single-volume history of the whole movement remains McBeth's *The Baptist Heritage*. That said, in common with many of the works noted above, McBeth gives too little prominence to anything beyond Britain and North America – the rest of the world is not ignored, but it is somewhat marginalized. More local histories are therefore often necessary. Unsurprisingly, the traditional homes of Baptist scholarship remain best served when we look for the local histories. In England, the Baptist Historical Society has published four volumes: White on *The English Baptists of the Seventeenth Century*; Brown on *The English Baptists of the Eighteenth Century*; Briggs on *The English Baptists of the Nineteenth Century* and Randall on *The English Baptists of the Twentieth Century*, which between them amount to a satisfying and full account. In America, the choice is wider and less clear-cut, but Brackney's *Baptists in North America* avoids the trap of focusing on only one strand of the diverse tradition better than most.

Continental Europe is beginning to get adequate histories, thanks in large part to the excellent work done at the International Baptist Theological Seminary in Prague. See, generally, Randall's *Communities of Conviction*, and Jones's *The European Baptist Federation*; see also, for some more specific stories, Jones and Randall (eds), *Counter-Cultural Communities*; and Pilli, *Dance or Die*. Ken Manley's work on Australian Baptist history seems destined to remain definitive for some time: *From Wooloomooloo to 'Eternity'* (2 vols). Much beyond this, however, the gaps are more noticeable than the areas of adequate coverage. However, two recent one-volume histories of the Baptist movement that deliberately attempt a global focus deserve mention: Bebbington's *Baptists through the Centuries* and Johnson's *A Global Introduction to Baptist Churches*. Both are admirable in intent and scope, though Bebbington's is perhaps the easier to read.

Full Bibliographic Details of Works Cited

Pushing at the Boundaries of Unity: Anglicans and Baptists in Conversation (London: Church House Publishing, 2005).

Baptism, Eucharist and Ministry (Faith & Order Paper 111; Geneva: World Council of Churches, 1982).

Beasley-Murray, George R., *Baptism in the New Testament* (Grand Rapids, MI: Eerdmans, 1962).

Bebbington, David W., *The Gospel in the World: International Baptist Studies* (Carlisle, PA: Paternoster, 2002).

—*Baptists Through the Centuries: A History of a Global People* (Waco, TX: Baylor UP, 2010).

Bosch, David J., *Transforming Mission: Paradigm Shifts in the Theology of Mission* (Maryknoll, NY: Orbis, 1991).

Brackney, William H., *An A–Z of the Baptists* (Lanham: Scarecrow Press, 2009).

—*A Genetic History of Baptist Thought: With Special Reference to Baptists in Britain and North America* (Macon, GA: Mercer UP, 2004).

—*Baptists in North America* (Oxford: Blackwell, 2006).

Briggs, John H.Y. (ed.), *A Dictionary of European Baptist Life and Thought* (Milton Keynes: Paternoster, 2009).

Briggs, John H.Y., *The English Baptists of the Nineteenth Century* (Didcot: Baptist Historical Society, 1994).

Brown, Raymond, *The English Baptists of the Eighteenth Century* (London: Baptist Historical Society, 1986).

Blau, Joseph L., 'The Wall of Separation', *Union Seminary Quarterly Review* 38 (1984), 263–88.

Bush, Russ, and Nettles, Tom J., *Baptists and the Bible (Revised and Expanded Edition)* (Nashville, TN: Broadman & Holman, 1999).

Clifford, John, *Inspiration and Authority of the Bible* (London: J. Clarke, 1892, 1895: 2nd Edition).

Colwell, John E., *Actuality and Provisionality: Eternity and Election in the Theology of Karl Barth* (Edinburgh: Rutherford House, 1989).

Cook, Henry, *What Baptists Stand For* (London: Carey Kingsgate, 1964: 5th Edition).

Cox, Samuel, *Salvator Mundi: Or, Is Christ the Saviour of All Men?* (London: Henry S. King, 1977).

Cross, Anthony R., and Thompson, Philip E. (eds), *Baptist Sacramentalism* (Carlisle, PA: Paternoster, 2003).

—(eds) *Baptist Sacramentalism 2* (Carlisle, PA: Paternoster, 2008).

Cross, Anthony R., and Wood, Nicholas J. (eds), *Exploring Baptist Origins* (Oxford: Regent's Park College, 2010).

Davies, Horton, *Worship and Theology in England: From Watts and Wesley to Martineau, 1690–1900* (Grand Rapids, MI: Eerdmans, 1996).

Early, Joe, Jr, *The Life and Writings of Thomas Helwys* (Early English Baptist Texts) (Macon, GA: Mercer UP, 2009).

Erickson, Millard J., *Who's Tampering with the Trinity: An Assessment of the Subordination Debate* (Grand Rapids, MI: Kregel, 2009).

Fiddes, Paul S., *Tracks and Traces: Baptist Identity in Church and Theology* (Carlisle, PA: Paternoster, 2003).

—*Participating in God: A Pastoral Doctrine of the Trinity* (London: DLT, 2000).

—*Past Event and Present Salvation: The Christian Idea of Atonement* (London: DLT, 1989).

—*The Creative Suffering of God* (Oxford: Clarendon, 1988).

Fosdick, Harry Emerson, *The Manhood of the Master* (London: SCM, 1916).

Garrett, James Leo, *Baptist Theology: A Four-century Study* (Macon, GA: Mercer UP, 2009).

Gill, John, *Body of Doctrinal Divinity* (3 vols; London: *s.n.*, 1769–1770).

Goodliff, Paul, *Ministry, Sacrament and Representation: Ministry and Ordination in Contemporary Baptist Theology, and the Rise of Sacramentalism* (Oxford: Regent's Park College, 2010).

Gordon, Adoniram Judson, *Ecce Venit* (London: Hodder & Stoughton, 1890).

Grenz, Stanley J., *Isaac Backus: Puritan and Baptist* (Macon, GA: Mercer UP, 1983).

—*Rediscovering the Triune God: The Trinity in Contemporary Theology* (Minneapolis, MN: Augsburg Fortress, 2004).

—*Theology for the Community of God* (Carlisle, PA: Paternoster, 1994).

Harvey, Paul, *Freedom's Coming: Religious Culture and the Shaping of the American South from the Civil War Through the Civil Rights Era* (Chapel Hill, NC: University of North Carolina Press, 2005).

Harmon, Steven R., *Towards Baptist Catholicity: Essays on Tradition and the Baptist Vision* (Carlisle, PA: Paternoster, 2006).

Henry, Carl F. H., *God, Revelation, and Authority* (3 vols) (Waco, TX: Word, 1976–1983).

Holmes, Stephen R., '*Religious Affections* by Jonathan Edwards' in Kelly Kapic & Randal Gleason (eds), *The Devoted Life: An Invitation to the Puritan Classics* (Downers Grove, IL: IVP, 2004), pp. 285–97.

—*The Holy Trinity: Understanding God's Life* (Milton Keynes: Paternoster, 2011).

—*Tradition and Renewal in Baptist Life* (Oxford: Whitley, 2003).

—*Listening to the Past: The Place of Tradition in Theology* (Carlisle, PA: Paternoster, 2002).

Hovey, Alvah, *Manual of Systematic Theology and Christian Ethics* (Philadelphia, PA: American Baptist Publication Society, 1877).

—*Manual of Systematic Theology* (Boston, MA: Silver, Burdett & co., 1892).

Johnson, Robert E., *A Global Introduction to Baptist Churches* (Cambridge: CUP, 2010).

Jones, L. Bevan, *The People of the Mosque: An Introduction to the Study of Islam, with Special Reference to India* (London: SCM, 1932).

Jones, Keith G., *The European Baptist Federation: A Case Study in European Baptist Interdependency 1950–2006* (*SBHT* 43) (Milton Keynes: Paternoster, 2009).

Jones, Keith G., and Randall, Ian M. (eds), *Counter-Cultural Communities: Baptistic Life in Twentieth-Century Europe* (Milton Keynes: Paternoster, 2008).

Lalleman, Pieter J., *Challenging to Change: Dialogues with a Radical Baptist Theologian. Essays Presented to Dr Nigel G. Wright on His Sixtieth Birthday* (London: Spurgeon's College, 2009).

Leonard, Bill J., *The Challenge of Being Baptist: Owning a Scandalous Past and an Uncertain Future* (Waco, TX: Baylor UP, 2010).

Luckley, H., *J. G. Oncken und die Anflänge des deutschen Baptismus* (Kassel: Oncken Verlag, 1934).

Lumkin, William L., *Baptist Confessions of Faith* (Valley Forge, PA: Judson Press, 1969: 2nd Edition).

McBeth, H. Leon, *The Baptist Heritage: Four Centuries of Baptist Witness* (Nashville, TN: Broadman, 1987).

McClendon, James, *Systematic Theology* (3 vols) (Nashville, TN: Abingdon, 1986–2000).

McDaniel, Charles, and Pierard, Richard V., 'The Politics of Appointments to Protestant Theological Faculties in Germany: The Case of Professor Erich Geldbach', *Journal of Church & State* 46 (2004), 55–82.

Manley, Ken R., *From Woolloomooloo to 'Eternity': A History of Australian Baptists* (2 vols) (Milton Kenyes: Paternoster, 2006).

Marsden, George M. (ed.), *The Fundamentals: A Testimony to the Truth* (12 vols in 4) (New York: Garland, 1988).

—*Fundamentalism and American Culture: The Shaping of Twentieth-Century Evangelicalism, 1870–1925* (Oxford: OUP, 1980).

Monck, Thomas, *A Cure for the Cankering Error of the New Eutychians* (London: *s.n.*, 1673).

Mullins, Edgar Young, *The Axioms of Religion: A New Interpretation of the Baptist Faith* (Philadelphia, PA: American Baptist Publications Society, 1908).

Payne, Earnest A., *The Baptist Union: A Short History* (London: BUGB, 1958).

Pilli, Toivo, *Dance or Die: The Shaping of Estonian Baptist Identity Under Communism* (Milton Keynes: Paternoster, 2008).

Randall, Ian M., *The English Baptists of the Twentieth Century* (Didcot: Baptist Historical Society, 2005).

—*Communities of Conviction: Baptist Beginnings in Europe* (Schwarzenfeld: Neufeld Verlag, 2009).

Randall, Ian M., Pilli, Toivo, and Cross, Anthony R. (eds), *Baptist Identities: International Studies from the Seventeenth to the Twentieth Centuries* (Milton Keynes: Paternoster, 2006).

Randall, Ian M., and Cross, Anthony R. (eds), *Baptists and Mission: Papers from the Fourth International Conference on Baptist Studies* (Milton Keynes: Paternoster, 2007).

Riley, William Bell, and Rimmer, Harry, *A Debate: Resolved, That the Creative Days in Genesis Were Aeons, Not Solar Days* (Duluth, MN: Research Science Bureau, 1929).

Robinson, H. Wheeler, *The Life and Faith of the Baptists* (London: Kingsgate, 1946).

Smith, Elliott, *The Advance of Baptist Associations Across America* (Nashville, TN: Broadman Press, 1979).

Spurgeon, Charles Haddon, *The Metropolitan Tabernacle Pulpit* (London: Passmore & Alabaster, 1856–1917).

Stovel, Charles, *Hints on the Regulation of Christian Churches...* (London: Jackson and Walford, 1835).

Strong, Augustus H., *Systematic Theology: A Compendium and Commonplace-Book Designed for the Use of Theological Students* (3 vols) (London: Kingsgate, 1907–1909).

Thompson, Philip E., 'Towards Baptist Ecclesiology in Pneumatological Perspective' (Ph.D. Thesis, Emory University, 2005).

Underwood, Alfred Clair, *A History of the English Baptists* (London: Carey Kingsgate, 1947).

West, Ellis M., 'Roger Williams on the Limits of Religious Liberty', *Annual of the Society of Christian Ethics* (1988), 133–60.

White, B. R. White (ed.) *Association Records of the Particular Baptists of England, Wales, and Ireland to 1660* (London: Baptist Historical Society, 1971).

—*The English Baptists of the Seventeenth Century* (Didcot: Baptist Historical Society, 1996: 2nd Edition).

Whitley, William Thomas, *A History of British Baptists* (London: Charles Griffen, 1923).

Williams, Roger, *The Bloudy Tenent of Persecution...* (London: *s.n.*, 1644).

Wright, Nigel G., *New Baptists, New Agenda* (Carlisle, PA: Paternoster, 2002).

—*Free Church, Free State: The Positive Baptist Vision* (Milton Keynes: Paternoster, 2005).

Zizioulas, John D., *Being as Communion: Studies in Personhood and the Church* (London: DLT, 1985).

Index